Differentiation
for
REAL
CLASSROOMS

To children of all cultures, all colors, all ages.
You are the world's greatest hope.

Differentiation
for
REAL
CLASSROOMS

Making it SIMPLE, Making it WORK

KATHLEEN KRYZA ~ ALICIA DUNCAN ~ S. JOY STEPHENS

CORWIN
A SAGE Company

For information:

Corwin
A SAGE Company
2455 Teller Road
Thousand Oaks, California 91320
(800) 233-9936
Fax: (800) 417-2466
www.corwinpress.com

SAGE Ltd.
1 Oliver's Yard
55 City Road
London EC1Y 1SP
United Kingdom

SAGE India Pvt. Ltd.
B 1/I 1 Mohan Cooperative
    Industrial Area
Mathura Road, New Delhi 110 044
India

SAGE Asia-Pacific Pte. Ltd.
33 Pekin Street #02-01
Far East Square
Singapore 048763

Printed in the United States of America.

Library of Congress Cataloging-in-Publication Data

Kryza, Kathleen.
Differentiation for real classrooms: making it simple, making it work/Kathleen Kryza, Alicia Duncan, S. Joy Stephens.
        p. cm.
Includes bibliographical references and index.
ISBN 978-1-4129-7246-8 (cloth)
ISBN 978-1-4129-7247-5 (pbk.)
    1. Individualized instruction. 2. Lesson planning. I. Duncan, Alicia. II. Stephens, S. Joy. III. Title.

LB1031.K78 2010
371.39'4—dc22   2009026778

This book is printed on acid-free paper.

09   10   11   12   13   10   9   8   7   6   5   4   3   2   1

Acquisitions Editor:	Carol Chambers Collins
Editorial Assistant:	Brett Ory
Production Editor:	Eric Garner
Copy Editor:	Alice Lanyk
Typesetter:	C&M Digitals (P) Ltd.
Proofreader:	Susan Schon
Indexer:	Judy Hunt
Cover Designer:	Michael Dubowe

Contents

List of Figures

Preface

As teachers we have a choice. We can choose to see our students' differences as an obstacle to reaching and teaching them. Or we can be joyfully curious, choosing to see the possibilities and the gifts that each student brings to our teaching and to our lives.

—Kathleen Kryza, Alicia Duncan, & S. Joy Stephens (2009, p. 2)

We are truly excited about the publication of our third book together, which is based on the C U KAN and chunk, chew, and check chapters from our first two books, *Inspiring Middle and Secondary Learners* (2007) and *Inspiring Elementary Learners* (2008). Our readers and the teachers we work with kept telling us that the C U KAN and the chunk, chew, and check framework made it easier for them to implement effective, differentiated instruction. When they asked for more, we said, "Okay, here it is!"

So the goal of this book is quite simply—keep it simple! Most of us already feel bombarded with the whirlwind of initiatives we are expected to address in today's classrooms such as Response to Intervention (RTI), Universal Design for Learning (UDL) and Understanding by Design (UBD), to name only a few.

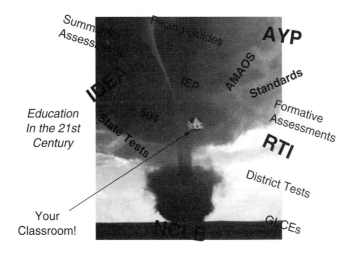

We created C U KAN and chunk, chew, and check as memorable and doable frameworks to support and transform our teaching from the chaotic frenzy that makes us feel like Dorothy when she rode the tornado into Oz to having that calm sense of inner knowing about our teaching that Dorothy had when she realized the power to get home was always inside her.

From these two frameworks we can create a clear vision of a classroom that is intentionally differentiated. The C U KAN framework helps us know where we are going. The CCC framework tells us how to get there. These frameworks help us to connect and simplify the UBD, RTI, and UDL initiatives into our classroom instruction (see Figure 0.1 for a schematic representation). Note that C U KAN provides a simplified framework for helping us design clear and meaningful targets for our lessons, while the CCC framework shows us where in our lesson to plug in the strategies to help students access the target.

FIGURE 0.1 Connecting Educational Initiatives to C U KAN and CCC Frameworks

Initiative	Intent	Data Needed	Questions to Ask	Making It Real 1. Identify your target 2. Know your students 3. Vary the pathways
Understanding by Design (UBD)	Intentionally teach standards and benchmarks in meaningful ways using a six page template	Student interests, readiness, learning styles, and preferences	How can we make learning meaningful for our students? How do we know if students are learning the understand, know, and able to do of a lesson?	**C U KAN:** Give it a go! Write clear and meaningful learning targets for the understand, know, and able to do on a one page template
Universal Design for Learning (UDL)	Intentionally provide access to information with multiple means: having flexible goals, methods, materials, and assessments	Student interests, readiness, learning styles, and preferences	Where in the lesson do we need to provide multiple means of access?	**Chunk, Chew, and Check:** Doable strategies, activities, and resources for planning multiple means of access during the input, process, or output of learning

Response to Intervention (RTI)	Intentionally address levels of learning differences and remediate learner deficits	What is working or not working for the student?	Where in the lesson do we need to address levels of learning and remediate learner deficits?	**Chunk, Chew, and Check:** Practical approaches to tier the chunk, chew, or check portion of a lesson

This easy-to-use, practical book will show how to—

1. Identify a clear learning target

2. Know your students, as people and as learners

3. Understand how to vary the learning pathways that will lead these many different learners to the same learning target

In Chapter 1 of this book, we refer to a lesson-planning framework we call the C U KAN framework, an acronym based on the following components—

- **Concept**: the big overarching idea of a unit or lesson
- **Understand**: the underlying principles that tell why the concept is important to learn
- **Know**: key facts and vocabulary
- **Able to do**: skills of the discipline that students need
- **Now you get it:** the way students demonstrate understanding (transfer) of the targeted learning objective

We use the C U KAN framework to develop clear, focused learning targets so that our lessons are relevant and rigorous for all learners, *and* also meet our state standards and benchmarks. (By the way, we like the name C U KAN because it inspires us to do the important work we do. *See, you can!* See, we *can* teach for meaning as well as teach to the standards and benchmarks. It's a joyful reminder that helps us improve the quality of our lessons.)

You'll notice that our chapters also begin with this acronym. It frames the content of each chapter as a teacher-learning target with the same components we use when creating lesson plans for students.

After clearly defining our learning target, we are then faced with the seemingly daunting task of helping very different learners reach that target. An important component in making this happen is to know and understand how different learners learn. We need to know our students as people *and* as learners. Chapter 2 offers ideas for getting to know our students and building a community that honors and accepts all learners. In Chapter 3 we define the second key framework that allows us to differentiate the pathways for all students to reach the same learning target. The chunk, chew, and check framework includes the following parts:

Chunk, (input): *Same learning target, different ways to* input *new information into learning brains.*

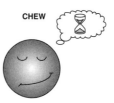

The brain learns best when it receives new information in small chunks. Because each brain perceives incoming information differently, we need to vary how we offer chunks of new learning.

Chew (process): *Same learning target, different ways for learners to* process *new information.*

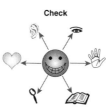

All brains have a unique way of connecting new information to what it already knows. Therefore, we need to offer students a variety of ways to chew on new information we have presented to them.

Check (output): *Same learning target, different ways for learners to* output *what has been learned.*

We know that individuals possess unique talents and therefore demonstrate understanding in their own way. We need to balance the ways we formatively and summatively check for student understanding.

Keeping the chunk, chew, and check framework in mind as we design our lessons will help us vary our teaching and offer better access to learning for all students in our classrooms. Every lesson, every day, we can begin to think this way:

"Chunk, chew, and check . . . it's how the brain learns best!"

Chapters 4 (chunk), 5 (chew), and 6 (check) offer dozens of practical ideas on how to vary lessons at both the elementary and the secondary level. Each of these three chapters includes the following:

- Ideas for varying that part of the lesson (chunk, chew, or check) by whole group, student choice/interests, and student readiness
- Ideas, strategies, and lesson examples that work for gifted, special education, and English language learners
- Technology ideas
- Lesson examples at elementary, middle, and high school

Finally, in Chapter 7, we show various ways to pull it all together: how to intentionally design differentiated lessons that weave in and out of chunk, chew, and check strategies and differentiate by whole class, choice, or readiness. We've included sample lessons at both elementary and secondary levels to use as a guide. (Keep in mind that our first two books are filled with lessons and rubrics to support you as you continue to grow your skills.)

Just as Dorothy and her friends followed the Yellow Brick Road one step at a time to lead them to the Great Oz and find their way home, if we approach our challenges one step at a time, we *too* will find our way home.

Dorothy has C U KAN and chunk, chew, and check in her basket of teaching tools to help her organize all her district initiatives

"You have plenty of courage, I am sure," answered Oz. "All you need is confidence in yourself. There is no living thing that is not afraid when it faces danger. The true courage is in facing danger when you are afraid, and that kind of courage you have in plenty."

—L. Frank Baum, from *The Wonderful Wizard of Oz*, 1900

Acknowledgments

We are fortunate to have Carol Collins as our editor, whose vision enabled us to make this book a reality. In addition, we are grateful for the production team of Brett Ory and Eric Garner, who supported and advised us as we completed the book.

We would like to thank Carol Ann Tomlinson, Grant Wiggins, and Jay McTighe, master teachers whose ideas and teachings have deepened our thinking and inspired our work in helping teachers differentiate instruction and teach for meaning. We would like to thank the many dedicated teachers and administrators we have worked with across the country whose willingness to take risks and venture onto new pedagogical paths continue to encourage and remind us that together we can and will create the change we wish to see in the world.

A special thanks to all the KIPP teachers we have worked with for the past four years for loving our chunk, chew, and check framework all along and for being some of the most inspiring, high energy teachers in the country. Work hard, be nice, and keep doing great things for kids.

Finally, we would like to thank our husbands—Roger, Noel, and Mark—whose loving support, encouragement, and patience is very much appreciated.

Corwin Press gratefully acknowledges the contributions of the following reviewers:

Allison Barnett
Social Science Teacher (Grades 7–8)
Caledonia Middle School
Caledonia, MS

Kathy Lineberger
School Library Media Coordinator
Marvin Ward Elementary School
Winston-Salem, NC

Salika Lawrence
Assistant Professor
William Paterson University
Wayne, NJ

Kathie Nunley
Corwin author of *Differentiating the High School Classroom*
Amherst, NH

Ernie Rambo
Teacher (Middle School)
Walter Johnson Jr. High School
Las Vegas, NV

Angela Schoenbeck
Clinical Instructor of Curriculum &
Instruction
Purdue University College of
Education
West Lafayette, IN

Jennifer Sinsel
Teacher (Science) (5th Grade)
Wichita Collegiate School
Andover, KS

Joseph Staub
Teacher (Resource Specialist)
Thomas Starr King Middle School
Los Angeles, CA

Rosemary Traore
Assistant Professor of Education
University of North Carolina at
Charlotte
Charlotte, NC

Thea H. Williams-Black
Assistant Professor
The University of Mississippi
Oxford, MS

About the Authors

Kathleen Kryza consults internationally for her company, Infinite Horizons, and also presents nationally for the Bureau of Education and Research (BER). Kathleen has more than twenty years experience in motivating and reaching children, educators, and others through her teaching, consulting, coaching, and writing. Her expertise is in working with students in special education, gifted education, alternative education, and multicultural education. She has a master's degree in special education and is an adjunct professor at University of Michigan Ann Arbor and Dearborn. Kathleen is also an active volunteer for the Challenge Day programs in Washtenaw County. She resides in Ann Arbor, Michigan, with her husband, Roger, and their "kids" Rennie (the dog) and Sasha (the cat).

Alicia Duncan is a consultant, program coordinator, and teacher trainer for the Waterford School District in Waterford, Michigan. She shares her expertise across the state of Michigan and throughout the nation in reaching and teaching English language learners, gifted students, culturally diverse learners, and inclusion students through differentiated instruction. She has a master's degree in ESL teaching methodology. She resides in Waterford, Michigan, with her husband, Noel, and their gifted (and challenging) feline companions, Henry and Harold.

S. Joy Stephens teaches two beautiful children (on a 24 hour basis!) to honor themselves as unique individuals. She has taught middle and high school students of all levels and abilities in differentiated science, math, and foreign language classrooms. She is a presenter and trainer in practical strategies for differentiating classrooms and inspiring students. She holds a master's degree in biology and resides outside of Memphis, Tennessee, with her husband, Mark, and two inspiring children, Alex and Susie.

Know the Target, Teach for Meaning (C U KAN)

Teacher Learning Target

Concept: Enduring understandings

Understand that (key principles)

- Teaching to conceptual understandings, as well as facts and skills, helps students make connections and see the relevance in what they are learning.

Know (facts)

- C U KAN lesson framework
- Intentional teaching
- Transparent teaching

Able to do (skills)

- Design learning targets based on the C U KAN framework and state standards and benchmarks.
- Teach transparently.

Now You Get It!

- Design one C U KAN lesson per quarter (see Resources for C U KAN planner) beginning with the units you teach that you know need the most work.
- As you teach the lessons, reflect on what you did that worked and what you would do differently.

If we want all learners to reach the same learning target, it is essential that we begin by designing a focused learning target. A focused learning target guides formative, summative, and student self-assessment and helps us design rigorous, meaningful lessons.

Our lessons become meaningful to students when we teach for understanding, not merely to impart facts and skills. (It's no secret that many students are not excited about learning facts and skills!) If we aren't intentional in showing them how the facts and skills connect to their lives, many students see the learning as irrelevant and become disengaged.

One challenge for us in designing meaningful lessons is that most state or district standards and benchmarks are a series of discrete facts or skills that don't seem to connect to one another. If *we* struggle to see the connections between these standards and benchmarks, how can we expect students to see the connections? Another challenge for us is today's textbooks. They cover way too much content and can't effectively be used as a guide for designing clear learning targets. However, once we know our target, we can not only see where the textbook can be used as a tool to teach to the target but we can also be open to the many other options from which our students can take in content.

To help create a clear learning target, we have created a lesson design framework we call C U KAN. It ensures that lessons teach for understanding, are rigorous and meaningful, and also reach district standards and benchmarks.

WHAT IS C U KAN?

We like to pronounce it *See you can!* to help us remember the important components of meaningful lessons. C U KAN is an acronym for components that are essential to creating meaningful lessons (see Figure 1.1). When planning a unit or lesson, the C U KAN framework helps us clarify the objectives, or learning targets, for the lesson. Our framework is adapted from the work of Carol Ann Tomlinson and Jay McTighe (2006).

FIGURE 1.1 C U KAN Components

CONCEPT

The **concept** is the big overarching idea of a unit or lesson. The concept is *not* the topic of the lesson, such as "consonant blends" or "subtraction." It is very global, broad, and can be applied across subject areas. The concept is usually one word such as *change* or *relationships*. At the elementary grades, teaching to a concept will allow you to design thematic units.

UNDERSTAND (that)

The **understandings** are the underlying principles embedded within the concepts. Understandings answer the question, "Why is it important to know this?" and help us connect the content to students' lives. When developing understandings for our lessons, adding the word *that* ("Understand that . . .") helps us move away from teaching just facts and knowledge toward teaching the big ideas that are the heart of our subject, such as "Understand that change happens over time."

KNOW

The **know** includes the key facts and key vocabulary that enable students to speak to the understandings. They are often examples of the understandings or facts related to the understanding. The facts are content specific such as, "Michigan has shores on three of the Great Lakes" or "The main characters in *Charlotte's Web* are Charlotte and Wilbur."

ABLE TO DO

The **able-to-do** skills are the social skills, production skills, fundamental skills, or skills of the discipline that students need to be able to do as they work toward the understandings. **Able-to-do** objectives might be "able to work in groups," "able to read a chart," or "able to create a graphic organizer."

NOW YOU GET IT!

The **now you get it!** is the way that students demonstrate understanding (transfer) of the targeted learning objectives. The **now you get it!** can occur during and after learning by using exit cards, tests and quizzes, and various performance-based assessments.

WHY C U KAN?

When we use the C U KAN framework, designing engaging and meaningful lessons becomes more effective and efficient. The C U KAN framework lets us begin with the end in mind and helps us do the following:

C U KAN provides a clear, relevant learning target.

For us—The more clear we are about the learning target we need students to reach, the easier it becomes for us to focus on what we want to accomplish. Then we can design lessons that connect to our students and their world. The C U KAN framework helps us point out global applications, underlying principles, and essential information that make learning relevant for students.

For our students—Our students want to know and deserve to know how the content we teach connects to their world. The C U KAN framework allows us to give a meaningful response to the question, "Why do we have to know this?" We will be able to respond to students by explaining things such as, "Good readers have a toolkit of strategies that help them make sense of text. Today, we are going to add another important tool to your toolbox so that you can become a better reader." With meaningful learning targets, students will know how the learning connects to their lives.

C U KAN guides us to more meaningful instructional methods.

For us—Being clear about the learning target before we write our daily lessons ensures that the activities we design are really hitting our target and are not simply busywork. A clear learning target helps us plan instructional options that reach all our students. For example, we can plan for students who need information visually, students who learn best through discussions, or students who need language support. The C U KAN framework also frees us from teaching to the book. It helps us discern what parts of the book support the learning target and where other resources would better hit the target. For example, we don't need to teach ten vocabulary terms just because our textbook has printed them in boldface type in Chapter 3. A clear learning target allows us to make better choices about which words our students most need to know in order to deeply understand, apply, and transfer the learning.

For our students—How can students possibly select a learning strategy to help them hit the target when they don't know what the target is? When the learning target is clear, our students can shift their thinking from "What am I supposed to be learning?" to "What is the best way for me to learn this?" A clear learning target allows students to use their time more efficiently by studying in a way that works for them.

C U KAN provides a target for meaningful, ongoing assessment.

For us—Our assessment options become clear when we ask, "How can students best demonstrate that they understand the learning target?" When we know our target and we know our students, we can better determine whether to offer choices, tier our lessons, or let students do independent learning contracts. We can also save ourselves valuable class time by preassessing to determine what our students already know or don't know about the learning target. This information helps us to prioritize our time and focus on what students really need to learn.

For our students—Clear learning targets help our students reflect on and assess their own learning growth. Posting the learning target where students can clearly see it will continually remind them where they are going. When students know where they are going, they can assess what they have mastered and what they have yet to learn.

C U KAN EXAMPLES

Figures 1.2 and 1.3 show examples of the concept, understanding, knowledge, able to do (skills), and now you get it! framework for several different content areas. See Resources for other examples of understandings in various subject areas and grade levels that will serve as models for writing lessons.

Following these charts, you will find a detailed example of a weeklong lesson plan on heroes developed using the C U KAN model (Figure 1.4, page 7). The C U KAN framework can be used for longer projects, like this example, but it can also be used for short one-day lessons, homework, or even ongoing class work. The learning target guides the teacher through each component of lesson planning. It also appears at the beginning of the student handout as a reference and reminder of the learning target (Figure 1.5, pages 7–8).

FIGURE 1.2 Secondary Sample Learning Targets

	Social Studies	Science	Math	Language Arts
CONCEPT *The big idea of a unit/lesson, usually one word*	Systems	Systems	Number Sense	Purpose
UNDERSTAND *What is the principle or concept that you want students to understand? (Should be global, relevant, and have broad applications.)*	Understand that a democratic government maintains a system of checks and balances so that no one way of thinking can take over	Understand that a decrease in habitat contributes to a decrease to the population of local species	Understand that everything is made up of wholes and parts	Understand that writer's use persuasive techniques to convince others of a point of view
KNOW *What are the key facts and key vocabulary words that you want students to know?*	Fascism Hitler Goering Allies Major events and dates that led to WWII	Contributing factors to habitat destruction Habitat conversion Predation Endangerment	Numerator Denominator Equivalent fractions	Types of persuasive communication techniques
ABLE TO DO *What basic skills, social skills, production skills, and/or skills of the discipline will students be able to do as a result of this lesson?*	Read and comprehend text Take notes Work in groups	Research via field study or online investigation Comprehend text Gather data Interpret data	Compare whole numbers and fractions Multiplication Division Work independently	Brainstorming Rough drafts Revision and editing techniques Make a goal and create a plan to follow through
NOW YOU GET IT! *How could students demonstrate their understanding?*	RAFT Plus (see Chapter 6): Role play from the perspective of a historical figure we studied	Choice menu Letter to the editor Data display with conclusions Public service announcement Children's book	Tiered lesson a. Create fraction strips at varying levels of complexity b. Create story problems from your life that show understanding of wholes and parts	Interest-based groups Analyze writing models, then write a persuasive piece

FIGURE 1.3 Elementary Sample Learning Targets

	Social Studies	Science	Math	Language Arts
CONCEPT *The big idea of a unit/lesson, usually one word*	Community (Second grade)	Force (Fifth grade)	Time (First grade)	Language (Kindergarten)
UNDERSTAND (that) *The underlying principle that connects the content to students' lives*	Understand that in a community there is an interaction between the people and the natural environment	Understand that humans study how nature works and use that knowledge to create things that make life easier for humans	Understand that people made up the idea of time as a way to measure how long events or actions take place and so they could organize and plan	Understand that humans created a system of sounds and symbols so that they could communicate effectively
KNOW *The key facts and key vocabulary words that support the understandings*	The natural and human characteristics of where we live	Six types of simple machines Force, distance, work	Hour Half hour Half past the hour	Each letter of the alphabet produces its own sound The sound of each letter is the code that allows humans to communicate
ABLE TO DO *The basic skills, social skills, production skills, and/or skills of the discipline students will be able to do to work toward the understandings*	Use graphic aides like maps or pictures Gather data about our community	Create a compare/contrast chart that shows the different types of simple machines Calculate the amount of work *(F × D = W)*	Tell time to the hour and half hour	Identify the letters of the alphabet and their sounds
NOW YOU GET IT! *How students demonstrate their understanding of the above learning objectives*	RAFT Plus: Role play a person from the community and tell how you interact with the environment	Centers: Students rotate through six centers, one on each machine. They complete activities and the compare/contrast chart.	Tiered lesson: Tier 1: Students work on telling time with a digital or analog clock Tier 2: Students create a daily schedule for a typical school day	Choice: Students choose one activity/center from a choice menu that is posted on the whiteboard for them to see

FIGURE 1.4   C U KAN Lesson Design

C U KAN Lesson Design

Name:	**Grade Level of Lesson:**

CONCEPT: Relationship   **TOPIC:** Heroes

As a result students should. . .

Understand that (key principles)

- We learn about how we want to lead our lives by studying the lives of people who have had a positive impact in the world.

Know (facts)

- Hero characteristics
- Heroes—past and present

Able to do (skills/be able to. . .)

- Select someone who is a hero to you.
- Collect characteristics of that person that you admire.
- Present information about your hero.

Preassess: How will you determine students' readiness, interests, or learning profiles before starting your lesson/unit?

Quick Write Exit Card—Do you have a person that you admire or look up to? If yes, who is that person, and what do you admire about them? If no, list qualities you respect or admire in others.

FIGURE 1.5   Sample Student Handout

Hero Choice Menu

Concept: Relationship

Understand that (key principles)

- We learn about how we want to lead our lives by studying people who have had a positive impact in the world.

Know (facts)

- Hero characteristics
- Heroes—past and present

Able to do (skills/be able to . . .)

- Select someone who is a hero to you.
- Collect characteristics about that person that you admire.
- Choose a way to present information about your hero and your hero's impact on your life.

(Continued)

FIGURE 1.5 (Continued)

Present a skit or video about your hero and how that person impacted life.	Write a story about how you changed your life because of what you learned from your hero.
Make a chart comparing your future life with your hero's life.	Create a PowerPoint presentation about your hero's impact on your life.
Write and illustrate a book for younger children about your hero.	Write a rap/poem/song about your hero.

HOW TO WRITE A C U KAN

Below are some questions we can ask ourselves to guide the lesson-designing process using the C U KAN framework. The questions are a guide to help determine clarity as we create a concept, an understanding, facts (know), skills (able to do), or assessment (now you get it!).

When designing a *concept*, ask—

- Is the concept written in one or two words? (Concepts are one or two words, not phrases or sentences: for example, *patterns, systems, interrelationships, communication.*)
- Is this a concept or a topic? Topics are specific to what is being taught: a life cycle, fractions, *To Kill a Mockingbird*, the American Revolution. Concepts are big, global ideas that could be taught again and again, such as patterns, relationships, systems, or communication.

When designing the *understanding*, ask—

- Could this idea be taught and used in several contexts in my content area? For example, in math, you might have the following understanding:
  - *Understand that everything in the world is made up of wholes and parts and mathematicians have found numerical ways to represent this that can be used in real-life applications.*
  - This understanding could be used over and over again when teaching fractions, decimals, ratios, percentages, and more.
- Is there an example of this idea that could be applied to other content areas? For example, "Understand that change happens over time. This *understanding* could be connected and taught in any subject area at any grade level because change happens in science, math, social studies, language arts, and other areas of learning.
- Is this a global statement that could be connected and made relevant to students' lives? For example, when teaching about how change happens

over time, we can begin the unit by making connections to how the students themselves or their work is changing over time.

- Did I write the topic for my lesson into the understanding? If so, it's not global enough. For example, if you write, "Understand that fractions are a way to represent wholes and parts," you can use that *understanding* only during a unit on fractions. The scope is too limited, and that limits the connections you can make.
- Does the understanding guide students to think like scientists, mathematicians, writers/readers, or historians?
- Would I more likely need to evaluate this part of the learning target by asking students to do a performance-based assessment, such as an essay question, project, or simulation? *Understandings* do not usually lend themselves to true/false or multiple-choice questions.
- Is the statement written, "understand that" rather than "understand why" or "understand how"?

When designing the *know*, ask—

- Is this a specific fact?
- Is this a key vocabulary word?
- Is this an example of something?
- Could I test this information with a true/false, multiple-choice question?

When designing the *able to do*, ask—

- Is there an action involved?
- Would students have to do something?
- Would students benefit from having something demonstrated to them in order to do this?
- Would I assess this by asking students to do or demonstrate a skill?

When designing the *now you get it!* ask—

- Are students being asked to show or demonstrate what they have learned?
- Is this a formative or summative activity?
- Are students expected to self-reflect or self-assess?

C U KAN AND PRIMING THE BRAIN: MAKING CONNECTIONS

Once we have designed a clear learning target, we can begin our units by connecting what we are about to teach to students' lives. Using the language of brain research, we can *prime* students' brains to get them ready to learn the new content since the learning brain always seeks to make connections (Jensen, 1994).

For example, in the sample lesson on heroes, the *understanding* reads, "Understand that we learn about how we want to lead our lives by studying the lives of people who have had a positive impact in the world." To help students connect to this understanding, we may choose to prime their brains by sharing examples of our personal heroes, explaining why we admire those heroes, what we learned from them, and how that has impacted our life choices. This connection to our own lives helps students make connections to the heroes in their lives. If an *understanding* in language arts is, "Understand that writers have a toolkit of strategies they use to communicate effectively. The greater the toolkit of strategies, the more choices the writer has for reaching varied audiences," we could begin our lesson on the importance of punctuation marks by reading the book, *Eats, Shoots & Leaves: Why Commas Really Do Make a Difference!* by Lynne Truss (2006). This *prime* makes a point by using humorous examples that connect readily to students' lives.

We can prime students' brains with video clips, PowerPoint presentations, models, and real-life examples. When we take the time to prime students' brains and set the stage for what's to come, we keep a sense of curiosity and wonder alive in our classrooms.

C U KAN AND ONGOING ASSESSMENT

Beginning with a clear learning target also guides assessment, from preassessment through formative assessment to summative assessment.

When we preassess, we determine whether it would be helpful to have information about the understand, know, or able-to-do part of our learning target. For example, in the hero lesson, we would probably want to know if students have heroes and if they can name traits they admire. This gives us information about students' understanding of the idea of heroes and what they know of hero characteristics. When preassessing a unit on adding fractions, we would most likely want to pretest students' able-to-do skills.

Because we are clear on our target at the beginning of our units, we are clear regarding what we need to formatively assess throughout the unit. We can also share the target with students and have them self-assess throughout the learning process. For example, once students are working on their chosen projects for the hero lesson, we can ask them to complete exit cards to reflect on how well they have included the required learning targets in their project and what they still need to include (see Figure 1.6). The exit card helps the students own their responsibility for working toward the learning target and allows us to formatively assess student progress along the learning path. We can then provide additional support or additional challenge for students as needed.

Finally, starting with a clear C U KAN learning target helps us determine what the summative assessment should look like and what it should include. For example, when designing the hero lesson project, the summative assessment is the project. Based on the learning target, there is no need for a traditional test or quiz because that is not the desired outcome for the lesson. However, when assessing a skill like adding fractions, a quiz or test makes the most sense. From a clear target it becomes easier to see what we could learn with a traditional test or quiz or what would be better assessed through something like an essay question or

FIGURE 1.6 Hero Exit Card

Hero Self-Assessment Exit Card

Assess yourself on the learning target for your hero project:

A. On a scale of 1 (low) to 5 (high), how well does your choice project show your understanding of your hero's positive impact on your life?

1 2 3 4 5

B. Do you think you included enough specific characteristics and examples about your hero to make your project powerful?

1 2 3 4 5

C. How would you rate the quality of your project at this time?

1 2 3 4 5

What steps do you plan to take on your project before the due date?

student-designed project (a visual display, skit, song, or model). Summative assessments may often end up being a combination of more traditional assessments of facts and skills as well as activities such as an essay question or visual representation that evaluate deeper understanding.

When assessing a project, the advantages of starting with a clear learning target become obvious. Because we have already established our criteria, designing a rubric for the final assessment is easy. Look at Figure 1.7, the rubric for the hero lesson. Note how the learning target becomes the criteria for assessment. This allows us to design only one rubric, even though students are choosing from several projects. Figure 1.8 shows how an early elementary rubric would look. When using the rubrics, first the students self-assess on the rubric, and then the teacher does the final assessment using the same rubric. The students don't give themselves points; they mark an "X" where they think they performed for each target in the rubric.

FIGURE 1.7 Secondary Hero Lesson Rubric

Hero Rubric

Name _____   Project Choice _____

Expectations	Excellent	Good	Okay	Needs Improvement
Understands that a hero can impact how you will lead your life ___ Points				

(Continued)

FIGURE 1.7 (Continued)

Expectations	Excellent	Good	Okay	Needs Improvement
Knows facts about a hero's life ___ Points				
Quality work (As self-defined) ___ Points				
Questions and notes ___ Points				

Two ways I/we will do quality work for our project

1. _____

2. _____

What I did that was quality work:

_____

What I could do better next time:

_____

Teacher comments:

FIGURE 1.8   Elementary Hero Lesson Rubric

Hero Rubric

Name: _____   _____

Project Choice: _____

How I Did	😊	☹
Understands that we learn how to be a good person by studying other good people		
Knows what good things you admire about a hero		
Good project (Quality Work)		

What I did that I am really proud of:

_____

What I could do better:

_____

Teacher comments:

HOW C U KAN WILL HELP US DIFFERENTIATE

The C U KAN framework helps us differentiate because it provides a clear map for what we want our students to understand, know, and be able to demonstrate. C U KAN also helps us design an aligned rubric that focuses on the essential learning points. We know what we are looking for and what it looks like when students get there.

C U KAN gives us the road map to begin differentiating:

1. How students take in the C U KAN information *(Chunk)*

2. How students process the C U KAN information *(Chew)*

3. How students demonstrate their understanding of the C U KAN *(Check)*

We can readily convey the importance of content to our students when we have a clear learning target to aim toward and when we make real-life connections to that target. Sharing the learning target encourages students to take responsibility for their own learning. They are able to self-reflect; they know when they are getting or not getting the targeted objectives. Starting with a clear learning target also allows us to think of alternative options for assessing and reporting students' progress toward learning outcomes.

C U KAN helps us make our teaching more intentional and transparent (see Figure 1.9). Intentional teaching is when *we* know why we are teaching what we are teaching. Teachers who are clear on their learning target can be more intentional because they can use the target to guide them as they make choices about what is most important to teach, and why. For example, Gayle was really excited and ready to teach students through varying multiple intelligences, so she designed a lesson in which her seventh-grade students could get in

FIGURE 1.9 Intentional and Transparent Teaching

Intentional	Transparent
You collect data on a survey about your students' learning styles or multiple intelligences *because* you want to find out how your students learn best so you can design lessons that work for them.	You explain to students that you will be teaching vocabulary to varying learning styles, so they can self-assess which learning style works best for them in order to be more effective at studying and learning.
You model quality use of sustained silent reading (SSR) time *because* you believe in the value of reading with your students. You get excited about the book you are reading. Read intently. Share and talk about books students are reading.	You ask students to create a list of quality uses of SSR time versus poor uses of SSR time. Then students create a bulletin board of pictures of students modeling quality versus poor behaviors. You explain to students that they must ultimately own their own reading lives and they can develop behaviors that develop lifelong reading.
You give a performance-based assessment rather than a test to have students show their understanding of the similarities and differences between the cultures in Asia and in America today *because* you know this will assess for a deeper understanding than you would see on a test or quiz.	You explain to students that the reason you will assess using a performance-based project rather than a test is that you want to see their understanding of cultural connection, not just their knowledge of the facts.
When checking homework in math, you have several students think aloud the varying ways they got to the correct answer because you want students to model for each other that there is more than one way to get a correct answer in math.	When students share another way to get to the correct answer, you note it out loud to the class. "Great, Amir, that is indeed another way to get to the same answer. How many of you can see how Amir came up with his answer?"

multiple-intelligence groups and use their intelligence strength to learn the major bones in the body. However, if Gayle had planned her C U KAN first, using district standards and benchmarks for seventh grade, she would have realized that there is no benchmark that requires students to know the bones in the body. However, they do need to be able to demonstrate how bones are part of an interconnected system. Because she didn't have a clear learning target, she wasn't intentional. Her lesson would have been engaging for students, but it was not rigorous. Because she wasn't being intentional, Gayle's lesson was essentially busy work.

Transparent teaching is when *the students* know why we are teaching what we are teaching. Transparent teaching is teaching *with* the students, not *at* them. For example, an able-to-do skill that Heather has in her C U KAN target is on gathering information and determining important from interesting information. When Heather teaches a new processing (chew) strategy to her students, she always explains to students why she is teaching them the strategy and how the strategy can help them in school and in life. For example, when she teaches a note-taking technique, she first talks to students about how important note taking is as a lifelong learning tool for helping learners to gather and process (chew) their learning. She explains how they will not only need to be note takers throughout their schooling, but they also will be taking notes as adults when they are building a house or buying a car or planning a wedding. She explains to them that she will be taking time to think aloud, model, and scaffold the instruction of a note-taking technique that they will be using throughout the year so that when they leave her class, they will own a note-taking technique that they can use for the rest of their lives if they choose. Transparent teachers, like Heather, help students see the ownership and accountability they have in the learning process.

Designing lessons using the C U KAN framework may seem challenging initially, but once we use it consistently, we find that it ultimately makes our teaching more efficient and effective.

2

Know the Learners, Build Relationships

Let us think of education as the means of developing our greatest abilities because in each of us there is a private hope and dream which, fulfilled, can be translated into benefit for everyone and greater strength for our nation.

—John F. Kennedy, President

Teacher Learning Target

Concept: Learning profiles

Understand that (key principles)

- Teachers who recognize their students' learning styles are able to design more effective instruction that moves learners toward the same learning target (Chapter 1).

Know (facts)

- Learning profiles
- Learning styles

Able to do (skills)

- Use surveys to gather data.
- Organize data in user friendly formats.

Now You Get It!

- Choose one survey to conduct (see Resources) in the next month. On a sticky note, jot down three things that surprised you about your learners. Place it in a prominent place as a reminder of the importance of getting to know them and determine how you will use that information to inform your instruction.

All children bring unique life stories with them when they walk through our doorways. If we pay attention, we can learn much from their stories. We see students who are wearing the same clothes day after day. We watch students struggle with peer pressure and bullying. We see young people raised by grandmothers or not really raised by anyone at all. We see students who are constantly pushed by parents to always be the best. The stories our students bring to class are an integral part of their humanness. Understanding and having compassion for our students' stories is essential to building a classroom community where students feel safe. When we take the time to get to know our students as people and as learners, they are more likely to trust us and respect us. Only then do we stand a chance of opening the pathway to the one thing we know can help them overcome the challenges they face—an *education*. Research reminds us that the characteristics of a teacher are just as significant as the attributes of a student's background (Wenglingsky, 2002). The power teachers have to shape students' lives is immense; the possibilities are inspiring. The more intentional we are about getting to know our students, the more effective we can be in reaching them in our classrooms.

GATHERING DATA

Taking time to learn about our students prepares us to connect learning targets to their lives (through their interests and hobbies) and helps us design lessons that are engaging and meaningful (by teaching to varied learning-styles and readiness levels). The most efficient way to learn more about our students is by collecting data through surveys, questionnaires, and inventories. Figure 2.1 shows examples of data to collect about students. You can find reproducible surveys in the Resource section of the book or you can download and customize them from our Web site, www.inspiringlearners.com.

FIGURE 2.1 Collecting Data About Students

Data	What It Is	How to Collect It	Use It For
Academic scores	Grades, standardized tests, pretests	Student records, formal and informal observations, test scores	Working with students by readiness levels
Learning preferences	Preferences students have regarding their learning environment	Learning preference surveys, student interviews, journaling prompts, discussions	Changing the physical environment to offer choices for how students work: on the floor, walking around, near a window, soft music playing, and so on

(Continued)

FIGURE 2.1 (Continued)

Data	What It Is	How to Collect It	Use It For
Learning styles	The way in which a student chunks, chews, and checks new information	Multiple intelligences surveys, Sternberg's intelligences surveys, learning style surveys, kid watching	Informing instruction to adapt to varying learning styles, grouping students by similar or varied learning styles, offering assignment choices with specific learning styles in mind
Interest inventories	Noting students' general interests, attitudes they have about subject areas, or content-specific interests	Quick writes or quick draws, general and content specific interest surveys, class surveys, letter to the teacher, classroom discussion	Grouping students with similar interests, priming new learning by making connections to their interests, offering choices based on their interests

There are many, many different types of surveys available, including those in this book. You may be wondering, "Where do I begin?" At the start of the year, it makes the most sense to survey our students' learning strengths by giving them a learning style or multiple intelligence survey. These surveys give us information about what our students can do and like to do. We can use that information to help us design our differentiated lessons. As we grow our skills at collecting data about our students, we may decide to give a different survey each week for the first month of school to discover students' interests, learning preferences, and more.

The earlier in the year data are collected, the sooner we will have important information to guide our instruction. Not only will this information help us to make accommodations and differentiate according to students' needs, it will also send the message right from the start of the year that we care about who our students are as people and how they learn.

Kathleen's niece, an advanced learner, sent her the following e-mail at the beginning of her sophomore year in high school.

I like my science teacher a lot this year; he definitely has a different teaching style that I really like. I like the fact that he thinks out of the box. Mr. Sullivan did this interesting thing. He had us do a survey on what type of learners we were. I thought it was really cool the way he did it and how he tries to direct his class, addressing all types of learners. (Nina Kryza, age fifteen)

Our students clearly notice when we are interested in who they are. We build relationships when we pay meaningful attention to our students. If we wish to become a significant attribute in our students' lives, helping them overcome obstacles, we must build relationships of trust.

MANAGING AND USING THE DATA

For many of us, it is challenging to make the data easy to use and accessible when we have so many students in our classrooms. Developing a manageable system is essential if we are going to use the information when designing lessons, developing tests, or planning groups for cooperative activities.

Following are three examples of user-friendly formats teachers are using for gathering, managing, and using data about their students to inform and shape their instructional practices.

Ms. Santos, a kindergarten teacher, gathers data through *focused kid watching* for the first two weeks of school and thereafter. During center time and independent exploration, with clipboard in hand, she records her observations (Figure 2.2).

FIGURE 2.2 Excerpt From Focused Observation

Student	Work Habits	Learning Profiles and Strengths	Learning Challenges	Ways to Honor the Student's Learning Needs
Macie	Keeps to herself	Is focused, seems comfortable with own thoughts, loves art, self-smart	Doesn't participate in groups	Recognize her strengths, group her with others who are weaker in art; allowing her strengths to be an integral part of the project
Hunter	Is full of energy; bounces around	Tries to work but shifts focus often, enthusiastic, loves learning, full of ideas	Lacks confidence in his ideas	Use a timer for time on task to build stamina, help him reflect on his growth to build confidence
Jonah	Gets frustrated with "menial" tasks	Finishes work quickly and thoroughly, confident in his abilities, perceptive!	Does not communicate reasons for his frustrations	Tier assignments to challenge him more; teach him strategies for challenging himself

Ms. Santos compiled her data in one easily accessible place. She refers to it frequently during lesson planning and in preparation for one-on-one time with the students. Her data sheet serves as a reminder that Jonah needs strategies for challenging himself and Macie needs more opportunities to demonstrate her strengths in a group.

Mr. Waltzman used *tick marks* (Figure 2.3) to collect data about the learning preferences of his sixth graders. He compiled the data from each survey onto one that he laminated and keeps close at hand for reference.

FIGURE 2.3 Sample Survey: Environmental Learning Preferences

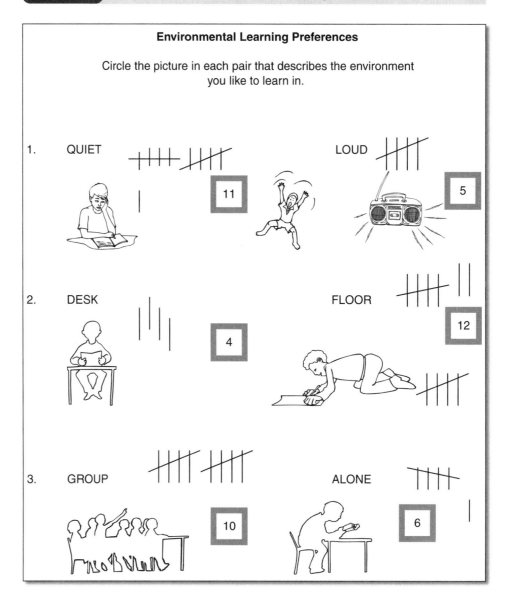

Mr. Waltzman was surprised to find out that twelve of his sixteen students preferred to work on the floor as opposed to sitting at the tables. With some hesitation, he allowed them to do so and was again surprised to find that these students got their work done much more effectively in a prone position! Mr. Waltzman also noted that five of his students liked a little noise when it came to *quiet processing* time. He grouped them together in one corner with some background music during review time and saw an immediate shift in attitude toward their work and performance.

Ms. Keller, a high school teacher, created a *learning-profile system* that she uses for better understanding her students. She uses 4 × 6 index cards and gathers several pieces of data during the first weeks of school. After students complete a survey, she has them summarize their findings on 4 × 6 cards. She then collects the cards and begins to add her own observations (see Figure 2.4). Teachers of younger students may need to transfer the data onto the cards themselves, but the effort is well worth it. Ms. Keller comments, "You know, it's sort of a pain to do the surveys and gather the data, but I now know about my students in September what I used to not know about them until April."

FIGURE 2.4 Learner Profile Card

Learning Styles	**Multiple Intelligences**

Modality

Interests / Hobbies

(Student's name on back of card)

Math Score

After reviewing the unit she was going to teach, Ms. Keller felt that students would learn and understand the vocabulary most effectively if they were placed with students of the same multiple intelligence. Pulling out her data index cards (Figure 2.4) the evening before class, she was able to arrange students quickly into art-smart, word-smart, body-smart, and music-smart groups. Students worked with others of the same intelligence strength to draw words, create word clues, do word charades, and compose word songs or rhymes. Students then shared their creations with others. Ms. Keller found that students who work with others of the same learning strength begin to internalize the learning and study skills that work best for them. Ms. Keller used the cards again to group students for a multimedia research project. She recognized that, this time, the final product was more creative when students worked with others who had *different* learning styles and strengths.

The way we gather information to better know our students varies from elementary to secondary. In early elementary, we can use simple word prompts and pictures to find out more about our learners. In upper elementary and middle school, students can read scenarios and complete traditional surveys. Further, secondary students can take a more active role in gathering the data and putting it into manageable forms, such as index cards or a class graph. What is most important is that we are intentional about gathering data about our learners' strengths and interests and that we manage the data so we can be proactive in meeting our students' needs.

Chapters 1 and 2 remind us of the importance of a clear learning target and a clear understanding of our students. Once we understand who our learners are, it becomes our responsibility to differentiate the pathways that will help all learners reach the same learning goal. The rest of this book is focused on the pathways to help all learners succeed—chunk, chew, and check.

3

Know the Pathways: Chunk, Chew, and Check

Once an individual knows something, he or she cannot unknow it. It follows that knowing obligates doing. Because we know better, we must create an environment that embodies the better that we know.

—Jamie Baker, Change
Leadership Consultant and Coach

Teacher Learning Target

Concept: Varying pathways

Understand that (key principles)

• Teachers vary the ways students acquire, process, and share new knowledge to cement learning in ways that are best for learners.

Know (facts)

• Chunk, chew, check (input, process, and output)
• Whole class, choice, tiering

Able to do (skills)

• Self-assess
• Use framework of chunk, chew, and check to offer varying pathways to learning

Now You Get It!

• Take out your lesson planner. Look at last Wednesday's lesson. Was there a clear chunk, chew, and check? If not, what stage needed to be added? Was there variation in your lesson for different learning modalities from the day before?

Chapters 1 and 2 remind us of the importance of defining clear learning targets and discovering and understanding what our students' strengths and needs are as learners.

With this knowledge, the need to differentiate becomes glaring. It is our responsibility to vary the pathways that will help our unique learners access the same learning goal. If we fail to differentiate, we are failing our learners.

More than ever before, we feel the pressures of many educational mandates that call for us to meet our students' needs. Response to Intervention (RTI) calls for us to evaluate how well our instruction is providing students with what they need. Is the child responding? How does the instruction and intervention need to change to help the child grow? Universal Design for Learning (UDL) calls for us to use all resources available to us, especially technology, to create open access for our students to acquire and process learning and demonstrate growth. Understanding by Design (UBD) recommends that we begin with the end in mind. Designing clear learning targets based on enduring understandings allows us to design lessons that are both rigorous and relevant to our students.

Educators contend with a virtual whirlwind of expectation, ideology, and terminology, all pointing to one idea: We must differentiate instruction if we are going to meet learners' needs. So the goal of this chapter is to show you how you can fit it all together in a practical manner with a doable framework we call "chunk, chew, and check" (CCC).

WHAT IS CHUNK, CHEW, AND CHECK?

Let's look at how this whirlwind of initiatives can be simplified into the CCC framework to create meaningful learning for all, starting with defining the terms.

1. Chunk/input—students acquire new information in varied ways.

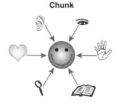

2. Chew/process—students make sense of new information in varied ways.

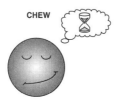

3. Check/output—students show what they have learned in varied ways.

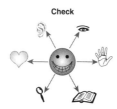

Varying these three steps in our lesson design allows us to respond thoughtfully to how well our learners gain access to content, process what we have taught, and demonstrate that they have mastered the outcomes. With the *CCC* framework in place, we can more carefully monitor where learning, or the demonstration of learning, is successful or where learning breaks down for the learner. This framework allows us to see how well students respond to the instructional interventions (RTI), it gives them access to content (UDL), and it allows us to move all learners toward the same learning outcomes (UBD). Best of all, by varying these three components of learning, we are creating joyful, successful, and meaningful opportunities for learning in our classrooms, thus molding a richer and more rewarding experience for our students and ourselves, as well.

WHY CCC WORKS

Teachers love the CCC framework because—

- Learners can relate to the language it uses.
  - When speaking with our colleagues and in professional settings, we may choose to use the terms *input* (or *acquire*), *process*, and *output*. When teaching students, however, we call these pathways *chunk*, *chew*, and *check* because it sticks. We use this terminology with kids to explain the learning process to them.

- It helps us be transparent in our teaching.
  - Teaching *with* our learners instead of *at* them means we include them in the learning process. When we teach transparently, our students know why we use certain strategies for learning. Making our teaching transparent with CCC might sound like this:
  - *"I am going to give you a* chunk *of new information for about ten minutes; then you will have time to* chew *on it with your talk partners because sharing ideas with another person is a great strategy for deepening your reasoning."*
  - After ten minutes—*"Okay, it's time to* check *your progress. Use thumbs up or thumbs down to indicate how you feel about this new idea. Do you get it? If you are still unsure, where can you go for help? Make a plan for the first few minutes of class tomorrow to clarify questions. Being self-reflective is something that everyone does to make sure they are on track because, let's face it, when you are an adult you often don't have a boss telling you what to do minute to minute. You have to start thinking, 'Do I know what I need to know?' and make a plan if you need help. So, let's continue to practice that."*

- It provides a road map for teachers to monitor themselves as they design lessons and activities. With CCC, we can determine where students are getting stuck. Do they need different access to the chunk? Is the chew not working for some? Is there a more effective way to check or assess student understanding (see "Planning for CCC")?
- It's a doable and meaningful way to incorporate into one useful framework that whirlwind of initiatives we deal with. For example, think about the engaging walk-about activity you learned in last Thursday's workshop. Would that be a great chew activity for your students? What about the English language learner (ELL) specialist's ideas for using hand signals to help struggling readers recall information? Yes, that would also be a great chew activity for not only your special education students but everyone in class. Have you learned about any new technology that would help students gain access (chunk) to new learning? What you should start to see is that many of the strategies you have learned over the years have a meaningful place in the CCC framework. Many of the best practices work for *all* learners, not just specific populations.

Students love the CCC framework because—

- Students can relate to its fun, catchy language.
- It helps students become better self-assessors. Knowing their learning target enables them to be aware that they should be monitoring the chunk, chew, and check of their learning and focusing toward that learning target. They can assess their progress by asking, "Am I able to take in a new piece of information? Is it locking in, in a way that sticks? Am I able to show that I got it?"
- It gives students the *why* of the content and the learning activities we teach. Because we are intentional and transparent (see Figure 1.9 on page 14), they will know why we do mind maps, why we use talk partners, why we put sticky notes in textbooks, why we assess in various ways.
- It allows students to advocate for themselves *"Ms. Douglas, can we chew on that a bit more because I didn't quite get it."*
- It empowers students to become lifelong learners. Outside of class and outside of school, for the rest of their lives, students will know how their own brains work best and have the tools they need to help themselves learn something new. Now how empowering is that?

CCC IN ACTION

Below is a snapshot of a coaching session. It is an example of how a teacher is learning to work with the CCC framework in a real classroom.

I was observing Sabrina as she presented a new math concept to her fifth graders. With great enthusiasm, she spent twenty-five minutes sharing all she thought kids needed to know about pie graphs. In the beginning, the kids were attentive, but I could clearly see that she had lost most of the kids after the first seven to ten minutes. However, because they were behaving, sitting in their seats, and not disrupting her delivery, she did not perceive that they were bored, disconnected, and disengaged.

Afterward, Sabrina and I sat down to reflect on the lesson. I shared with her several telltale signs I saw from my place in the back of the room that showed her students were not engaged in the learning.

Sabrina realized that she gave her students too big a chunk of new learning without giving them time to chew or process their understanding. The new information needed to be broken down into manageable amounts of time for chunking, with time to chew in between each chunk.

After reflection and discussion, Sabrina created the following lesson design for the same learning outcome, the relationship between circle graphs and percentages.

5 min	Chunk	*Teacher gives students circle-graph cutouts to explore.*
3–5 min	Chew	*Students discuss with turn-and-talk partners: How would a mathematician use these circles?*
10 min	Chunk	*Teacher explains how the graphs represent fractions.*
3–5 min	Chew	*Students do a problem from the book with table partners.*
3–5 min	Check	*Teacher walks around to observe students' progress with the new learning.*
10 min	Chew	*Teacher explains how the graphs represent percentages.*
3–5 min	Check	*Students work on a problem alone and then share with a partner.*
	Check	*Students complete a homework assignment.*

With time and experience, we find that when we teach in smaller chunks and give students more time to chew, our students are more engaged and they retain new learning. As we design our lessons keeping chunk, chew, and check in mind, we can build an indispensable toolkit of strategies to vary the ways students engage in meaningful learning.

Telltale Signs That We Are Not Being Heard (or Glaring Indicators That It Is Time to Chew)

- You see the tops of their heads, not their faces.
- Bodies are wiggling and moving.
- Other activities are going on, such as note writing, purse diving, or a thorough investigation of a pencil tip.
- Students are daydreaming, window gazing, clock watching.
- Their eyes are on you, but you see a glazed "look-through-you" focus.

PLANNING FOR CCC

Looking back over a week or two of our lesson plans, we may see clear delineations between the chunk, chew, and check. Often we find that chunk and chew blend (see Jigsaw activity in Chapter 4, for example), or it happens that one project is both a chew and check. No matter how we mix it up, the intent here is to vary the ways in which we have students input, process, and output new learning. If we design the chunk, chew, or check in the same way day after day (read the book, do the questions, and take the test, for example), we are not differentiating our instruction. *We* are responsible for creating the boredom, frustration, and apathy we see in our students. Here are some questions that guide our thinking and planning with the CCC framework:

- ✓ Are we offering different ways for students to chunk new information?

- ✓ Are we giving students ample opportunity to chew or process new learning in different ways?

- ✓ Are we asking our students to self-assess and reflect on what works best for themselves?

- ✓ When we check and see that some students are not "getting it," how does that shape or inform our instruction?

- ✓ Does this activity get my learners to the learning target? (The strategies must be more than fun; they must be meaningful.)

- ✓ How can I be transparent with my learners as I introduce this strategy? Will they understand *why* we are doing this?

LOOKING AHEAD

The remainder of this book includes chapters dedicated to the chunk (Chapter 4), chew (Chapter 5), and check (Chapter 6) framework. Within each chapter, we offer ways to differentiate by varying *whole-class* activities, by offering *choice*s based on learning styles or interests, and by *tiering* based on student readiness. Let's take a look at each way to differentiate and why each is necessary.

When we differentiate by whole class, we want to introduce the language of chunk, chew, and check and explain why each stage is essential for meaningful learning. We also want to expose our learners to different learning modalities and help them discover which learning style works best for them. By being transparent, our learners hear, *"We are going to chunk as a whole class today using a kinesthetic activity. Movement helps cement learning. Many of you will find this activity really helps you remember today's key points. Tomorrow we are going to try an activity for those of you who would rather see it to get it."*

We intentionally vary, from day to day, the whole-class modalities for acquiring, processing, and sharing new learning. Once we have worked with several modalities, we must *reflect* with our learners about which way worked best for them. We can do a show of hands or have students talk with someone else who learned best in a similar way. Students will be engaged and appreciate the varying styles. However, explaining why we all learn differently and encouraging students to use that information as a learning tool will propel them beyond appreciation and into personal empowerment.

Sometimes traditional whole-class instruction is simply the best way to deliver content. Traditional instruction is not taboo in a differentiated classroom. Delivery of new information might best be done as a whole-class "sit-and-get." Differentiating in real classrooms means we have the knowledge and confidence to make the instructional decisions that will best suit our students.

We can also differentiate the chunk, chew, or check part of our lesson by offering choices based on students' learning styles or interests. The power of offering choice in our classrooms should not be taken lightly. Think about it. Leaders understand the power of offering choices to their constituents. Skillful parents alleviate arguments with toddlers through the wisdom of controlled choice. Likewise, great teachers have known about the power of choice for years. Choice gives students a sense of personal control that is empowering. Learning how to make and follow through on choices is also key to a successful future. Our students need to know how to make good choices, and it will take time and hands-on guidance in the beginning as we explicitly teach them how to make good choices. Letting them fall when they make bad choices is OK, too! In failure, there is opportunity to reinforce reflection. We can say, "What about this choice didn't work for you? Why would you make a different choice next time?"

Finally, we can chunk, chew, and check by tiering lessons based on student readiness. Tiering the input, process, or output stage of learning allows us to adjust the difficulty level of material we introduce to students, the depth at which they are expected to process, or the complexity of their demonstration of learning. The key to planning CCC with tiering in mind is to think of varying depth and complexity of tasks expected of learners. We will share examples of getting started with two tiers. As tiering becomes more comfortable, we will give examples of ways to increase complexity of tiers based on student needs.

The next three chapters present many practical, doable strategies and ideas on planning and implementing the CCC framework in our classrooms, along with lesson examples for elementary, middle, and high school. These strategies work for *all* learners, but we note at the end of each chapter some specific considerations for gifted, special education, and ELL in each portion of the CCC process.

4

Chunk or Input

Multiple means of representation give learners various ways of acquiring information and knowledge.

— UDL Guidelines, Center for
Applied Special Technology, 1999–2008.

Teacher Learning Target

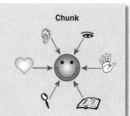

Concept: Chunk/input

Understand that (key principles)

- Teachers who vary learning modalities for teaching new information better meet the needs of the diverse learners in their classrooms.

Know (facts)

- Chunk (input)
- Learning styles
- Depth and complexity

Able to do (skills)

- Vary the modalities used to teach the chunk portion of lessons by whole class, choice, or readiness.

Now You Get It!

- Look back at your teaching each week and check to be sure you have used varied modalities for teaching new information to your students.

29

When we present new information, we can differentiate how students acquire, or chunk, the new information based on learning preferences, readiness level, and classroom circumstances. If we input new content the same way day after day, we are most likely not reaching all learners because we are not teaching to their preferred ways to take in information. The simple monotony of our instruction may also tend to make them disengage. Teachers who intentionally vary the way they input new information do so knowing that they are more likely to reach more learners and hold student interest.

CHUNK AS A WHOLE CLASS

Think about how we gather new information when we are planning a vacation. Generally, we don't look to only one source. We read books and brochures, go online, or talk to people who have been there. Gathering the information from varied sources is not only interesting, but it allows us to learn from different perspectives.

Similarly, when we differentiate the way our whole class takes in information, we want to make sure students receive that new information in various ways. Varying the chunk of a lesson by the whole class is a simple way to offer variety. It also requires less management because everyone is engaged in the same task. When we plan how students will access new information, it helps to keep the learning-styles framework in mind and think of our learners in terms of visual, kinesthetic, and auditory strengths by asking ourselves—

- What is another way besides reading the book that I can give students access to the information?
- How can I help them see, hear, or experience the new content?
- How can I use technology to help them access the content?

Whether we are reviewing problem-solving skills, teaching a new unit on place value, or discussing effective techniques that writers use, students benefit when they can take in the information in various ways on various days.

The following chart (Figure 4.1) is a general list of ideas for whole-class chunking of information according to different learning styles. Remember, this is how new information is getting into students' heads!

FIGURE 4.1 Chunk by Whole-Class Ideas

	Whole-Class Chunking or Inputting New Information	Visual	Auditory	Kinesthetic
Science	Students observe the cells of the organism they have dissected.	X	X	X
	Students listen to the teacher explain how to read the periodic table.	X	X	
	Students watch an elapsed-time video of a seed growing into a plant.	X		
	Students notice animal attributes from photos of animals.	X		
	Students listen to a passage from a text on tape while following along in the text.	X	X	
	A guest speaker shares information as an expert scientist.		X	
	Students investigate a model of how rocks are formed.	X		X
	Students learn information about mollusks through Tour de Chart (see below).	X		X
Social studies	Students watch a video clip from *The Patriot* to learn about the decisions that colonists had to make in getting involved in the Revolution.	X	X	
	Students gain new information by seeing a "big idea" board of all the topics they've studied connected by the big ideas or understandings.	X		
	Students listen to different cultural music from a region/country to learn about that region.		X	
	Students listen to/watch podcasts from varied political viewpoints.	X	X	

(Continued)

FIGURE 4.1 (Continued)

	Whole-Class Chunking or Inputting New Information	**Visual**	**Auditory**	**Kinesthetic**
	The class is addressed as "future community members" by a city or community council member.		X	
	Students look at a matrix that compares and contrasts the three parts of government.	X		
	Students learn about landforms through Take a Look! (see below)	X		X
Math	Students do an online Webquest to learn about inverse matrices.	X	X	
	Students describe the details of a bar diagram displaying survey results.	X	X	
	Students see various pictorial models of multiplication and division related to addition and subtraction in Chunk Stations (see below).	X		
	Students visit www.eduplace.com to study vertices of geometric shapes.	X	X	
	Students line themselves up by largest to smallest to learn the concept of greater than, less than.	X	X	X
	Students learn gestures that represent math functions.	X	X	X
English/ language arts	Students listen to an audiotape or watch a video of the story.	X	X	
	Students gain new information by seeing a vocabulary map for new vocabulary terms (how the word is used, what the word reminds them of, relationships, etc.).	X	X	
	Students put event cards in order before reading as a way to anticipate text.	X		X

Whole-Class Chunking or Inputting New Information	Visual	Auditory	Kinesthetic
Students notice the differences in sounds by looking at a chart of initial consonants.	✗	✗	
Students listen to a minilesson while looking at a sample-text lesson about the components of persuasive writing.	✗	✗	
Students scan a magazine article from *National Geographic Explorer* to identify text features such as headings, subheadings, and boldface print.	✗	✗	

Activities for Chunking as a Whole Class

Tour de Chart

Tell students to think of everything they know about the day's learning target. Then have all students jot down what they know on a piece of paper. The paper can range from regular notebook paper to large chart paper. When the time is up, all students post their charts on their bodies. Like walking billboards, students mill around the room in complete *silence* while reading others' charts. All students go back to their seats and add a few ideas to their own chart. Note that you will have to be sure that the information students have is correct information. Intentionally teach students that it's okay to make mistakes and that they should question the information if they think it may not be correct.

Take a Look

Post a collection of photographs related to the learning target in various locations around the class. For example, in geography, you could post pictures of natural landforms—plateaus, glaciers, and mountains. In math, you could post pictures of architecture that uses varied geometric shapes. Group the students into pairs. As if they are at an art exhibit, have the students walk and study the photos, either talking or jotting notes quietly. Allocate a set amount of time at each exhibit using a timer or music. When all students have observed every exhibit, select a chew activity for processing what they have seen.

Chunk Stations

Set up the room so that small groups of students rotate through chunk stations using varied modalities to learn key concepts. Stations can be set up for one or several days. For example, in one station students could watch a video. In another, they could read articles. A third station could be a technology station, and in a fourth the teacher or another expert could be there to discuss ideas. (Most stations are chunk and chew stations so students are also processing what they learn there.)

Visual Chunk Ideas

- Show a movie or clip from a movie.
- Demonstrate from a chart or graph.
- Create a PowerPoint.
- Read a book.
- Technology for visual chunking:
  - United Streaming, TeacherTube, BrainPop, Safari (see sites below):
    - Blog—Blogs contain individual commentary with subscribers' comments related to the posting.
    - Wiki—Used to create collaborative Web sites

Auditory Chunk Ideas

- Say it to the class (remember to present information in short chunks [about ten minutes] and give students time to chew in between).
- Play a song.
- Listen to a speech.
- Discuss information with each other.
- Technology for auditory chunking:
  - Listen to an audio recording or podcast.

Kinesthetic Chunk Ideas

- Do a role play.
- Demonstrate.
- Have students physically build something.

CHUNK BY CHOICE

Most of us have a preferred way to take in new information. For example, on our way to work or getting our day started, most of us catch up on local and national news. We may choose to listen to news on the radio (We even choose which station to listen to!), read news online, have a friend or family member fill us in, read the *New York Times* on the subway or even tune into *The Today Show* while flipping pancakes. We also make choices about what we take in as learners. Some of us tend to read fiction in our leisure time, while others choose nonfiction. We make such choices based on our passions, hobbies, and interests. In all of these cases, we are choosing how we *take in (chunk)* new information. The means by which we take in learning varies, depending on our preferences or even our circumstances.

Students appreciate being given choices on how they take in new content and what content they learn. Choice gives students a voice in our classroom and empowers them to make decisions that are good and right for them. Giving students choices is a fun and manageable way to differentiate the chunk of your lesson. Figure 4.2 offers examples of what chunk choice looks like. Note that you can offer as many choices as you want; whether it's two or twelve, it's up to you.

FIGURE 4.2 Chunk by Choice Ideas

	Choice 1	Choice 2	Choice 3
Chunk	Expert group: prepare a report about mammals.[a]	Expert group: prepare a report about reptiles.[a]	Expert group: prepare a report about amphibians.[a]
	Discuss in a group everything you know about ancient civilizations.	Read a short article about ancient civilizations.	
	Choose Short Story 1 to study internal conflict.	Choose Short Story 2 to study internal conflict.	Choose Short Story 3 to study internal conflict.
	Become a right triangle expert.	Become a scalene triangle expert.	Become an equilateral triangle expert.
	Students do an article exhibit in their core groups.[a]		

a. See the activity descriptions at the end of this chapter.

Activities for Chunking by Choice

Expert Groups

Expert groups can be formed in various ways to do a variety of tasks. Students work in interest-based groups determined by a preassessment (see Resources for a sample of content-specific interest inventory). Group members become experts in their area and are called upon throughout the unit to add bits of knowledge and expertise to class discussions. Each group shares with the rest of the class what its members have learned. The following are some examples of interest-based groups in content areas.

Science

Endangered species—Students are grouped according to the species they are most interested in studying.

Simple machines—Students are grouped according to the simple machine they are interested in exploring.

History/Geography

Colonial America—Students do an in-depth study of the group of their choice: Indians, British, the colonists.

Geography—Students become experts on the region they most want to explore during the geography unit.

English/Language Arts (ELA)

Literary circles—Students do book club literary circles to study books they have selected. The teacher could also present a lesson on a literary concept such as internal conflict. Students would then find examples of the literary concept in texts of their choice.

Writing genres—Students create magazines or newsletters by collaborating and contributing their choice of genre (e.g., feature story, advice column, recipes, editorials, etc.).

Math

Geometry—Students work in interest-based groups to study shapes of their choice.

Time—Students work in groups to brainstorm activities that can be done in different units of time: minute, hour, or day.

Health/Physical Education

Health awareness—Students collaborate in groups to learn about teenage health topics of interest.

Personal fitness—One day a week, students can form groups to participate in fitness activities of their choice (weight lifting, aerobics, jogging/walking, basketball, etc.).

Article Exhibit

On an assigned day, five students bring in an article related to the content the class is studying. The article can be from any news source or genre. Encourage students to look in publications they enjoy reading or related to their hobbies to help them make meaningful connections.

Students plan a variety of ways to share the information from their articles. One may explain an article with a diagram. Another might have the class read a portion of the article, then listen to an explanation. This assignment is motivating because it gives students ownership of their learning.

CHUNK BY TIERING

Think about where you are in your ability to work with new technology. Are you a digital native or are you, quite frankly, a little scared of all the new technology that's out there? In our work together, Alicia is the technology whiz. She is able to learn a new program by plunging in and testing it out. Joy is more inclined to read the manual to find out how a program works, while Kathleen must have another human being next to her showing her step by step what to do. Just like students in our classrooms, Alicia, Joy, and Kathleen have varied zones of proximal development and so need different entry points into new technology content (Vygotsky, 1978). They need the chunk of the lesson to be tiered.

We design a tiered lesson when we determine that our students need to take in information at various levels of complexity. As we plan, we think about how to make the information they need to know accessible at varied levels of depth and complexity. This means having new information available in formats that have more or fewer variables or that are more or less complex and abstract. (Think of the wide range in complexity of maps. Maps can be very straightforward, showing simple political boundaries, or quite complex, showing political boundaries as well as the topography of the land.) When tiering the chunk, it is important that we don't confuse giving less complex information with giving simpler work that is not aligned to our standards. All students should be required to learn the same information. (The exception would be a student who has a modified curriculum.) Conversely, we don't want to require more repetition of the same task for advanced students in the name of a challenge. What they require is more *complex* information, not *more* information. Figure 4.3 gives us an example of how a teacher might tier the input for students.

FIGURE 4.3 Chunk by Tiering Ideas

	Tier 1 (least challenging)	Tier 2	Tier 3 (most challenging)
Chunk		Students who didn't "get it," shown by preassessment with an exit slip, will work with the teacher to learn the math content.	Students who, after a preassessment with an exit slip, show they already know the content will do an enrichment activity extending the math strategy to more complex applications.
	Students will study a two-dimensional topographical chart with three landform characteristics.	Students will read a three-dimensional topographical chart that has five landform characteristics.	
	Varying texts: Students will read about animal characteristics in trade books written at a lower level.	Varying texts: Students will read about animal characteristics in the science text book.	Varying texts: Students will read about animal characteristics in advanced text from the Detroit zoo.

NOTE: See list of resources for varying text at the end of this chapter.

Activities for Chunking by Tiering

Gathering Tiered Text

- Begin gathering tiered text with the topics you teach that are the most difficult for students of varying abilities to understand (Shakespeare, for example). Find and add resources to this unit over time.

- When you have a topic that requires more tiered texts, try doing an Internet search. You will be amazed at the varied levels of text you will find. Adding *elementary* or *children* to your search will help you find lower-level or less complex text. The Internet is also a great resource for finding more advanced content on a subject. Look for authentic texts such as journal entries written by historical figures, real data from scientists, or reports written by researchers.

- Create a wish list of tiered text and present it to your PTA, or find and write grants to obtain materials of varied levels. The following are some publishers who have tiered materials:
  - National Geographic, K–12—theme sets
    - www.nationalgeographic.com/education
  - Time for Kids, K–12
    - www.teachercreated.com
  - Pearson AGS Globe, MS/HS—high interest, varied levels
    - www.pearsonschool.com

Jigsaw

- Form tiered groups with a low-, middle-, and high-level student in each. (You can have more than three levels if you choose.) Label each member of the group (Person A, B, or C).

- Each student in the group receives something to read related to the days' learning target. The reading material is tiered based on the readiness levels of individual student A, B, and C. You can print the readings on different colors of paper if you are using readings that are not from a textbook. If you are using text from books, you can assign passages of various levels of complexity.

- Students leave their *home* groups and meet in *expert* groups. (All the As meet together, the Bs meet together, the Cs meet together.)

- Expert groups read, discuss, and gather data from their reading (see the sample Jigsaw note-taking guide in Resources).

- The experts return to their home groups to teach their portion of the materials and to learn from the other members of the group (see Resources for a planning guide).

AutoSummarize

You can tier text yourself by scanning the desired copy into a Word file. Most word processors have a function called AutoSummarize. Typically it is in your toolbar, or you can search for it using your help menu. When you select Auto-Summarize, it will summarize the text for you! You can select the percentage you want to reduce the text for the summary (25, 50, or 75 percent). While AutoSummarize does a pretty good job of capturing the key ideas, be sure to read through the summary yourself and add any information students will need to reach the learning target. Also note that AutoSummarize does not change the reading level of the text, so you may need to simplify the language as well.

CHUNK: TECHNOLOGY SOURCES

- United Streaming/Safari/You Tube/Teacher Tube: Digital media sites (Google the names to link to these sites.)
  - Google Earth: Maps and Satellite Images. Google Earth and United Streaming have a joint project that offers teachers lesson plans and instructional suggestions.

- BrainPop: animated educational site
  - www.brainpop.com

- Wikispaces: Wiki building site
  - www.wikispaces.com

- Sites for tiering text or gathering tiered text
  - Prufrock Press—gifted education resources
    - www.prufrock.com
  - Free Spirit Publications—gifted education and special education resources
    - www.freespirit.com
  - Lerner Classroom—leveled nonfiction books, K–8
    - www.lernerclassroom.com
  - Recordings for the Blind and Dyslexic—books on DVD
    - www.rfbd.org
  - Reading A–Z—print leveled books
    - www.readinga-z.com
  - Natural Voices—scans and reads text
    - www.naturalreaders.com
  - Raz-Kids, K–6—online leveled e-books for kids
    - www.Raz-kids.com
  - ABC Read—self-taught phonics and spelling, great for ELL, lots of pictures!
    - www.abcread.com
  - UDL Editions by CAST—digital media for reaching and engaging all learners
    - www.udleditions.cast.org
  - CAST UDL Book Builder—create, read, and share engaging digital books that build reading skills for students
    - http://bookbuilder.cast.org Educational Synthesis—instructional resources on various subjects, for students from preschool to graduation and for regular ed, special ed, and gifted ed
    - www.educationalsynthesis.org

CHUNK: ACCOMMODATIONS

Gifted and Talented

- Gifted learners need the chunk to have more depth and complexity.
- Find more complex text online, from upper-grade texts, or from your own collection.
- While many students may need text that is at their grade level, gifted learners often appreciate and can handle primary source text. For example, they want to see and read the original Declaration of Independence and read actual scientific charts and graphs.
- Talented learners will be drawn to new information that is presented in unique ways, so activities like Tour de Chart and Expert Groups, will work for them.

Special Education

- If a student can't read the text, we have to find another way to help them access the chunk. Using audiovisual aides, simplified text, or text with pictures will help these students gain access to the required learning targets.
- Other student's summaries, organizers, or notes can be a great resource for special needs students. They can benefit from seeing other students' representations while discussing the content it represents.

English Language Learners

- Imagine being in another country where all the text is in a language you do not know. How would *you* access the content needed to get by? Just like you, ELLs need visuals, they need to be taught the meaning of key words, and they may need hand motions or movement to help them make sense of the content.
- ELLs need opportunities to say and use the words over and over again in meaningful context.
- Consider having peers summarize content information to an ELL followed by the nonnative speaker restating the summary back to their partner. This allows ELLs to get an extra opportunity to take in new information using the language of a peer.

CHUNK: LESSON EXAMPLES

An Elementary Application: Choice Expert Groups

In Ms. Hammerberg's second-grade class, students get to become experts on animals for the Animal Habitat unit. (She selected six animals based on the fact she had access to lots of reading materials about them. Not much available on aardvarks in the media center, don't you know!) Ms. Hammerberg gives her students a content-specific inventory that lists the topic choices. She has students rank their top three choices and assures them that they will receive one of the animals they pick. Ms. Hammerberg puts the students into groups who study and become experts on the learning target. Then they teach each other about their area of expertise. Students are engaged and enthusiastic about becoming experts and getting to teach their peers.

A Middle School Application: Whole-Class Chunk

Mr. Caffrey is teaching a unit on pollution. He has collected of variety of engaging ways for students to learn about the key concepts in the pollution unit. He has set up stations so groups of students can rotate through them during the week. In one station, he has various high-interest articles about pollution. In another, he has set up Web quests about pollution on three computers. In the third station, students watch a short video on pollution, and Mr. Caffrey, who volunteers at the recycling plant, is the resident expert at the fourth station. Not only do students enjoy learning in varied modalities, but they also get to move throughout the learning process, which keeps them alert and engaged.

A High School Application: Tiered Text

Ms. Lelle used to dread when it came time for the *Romeo and Juliet* unit in her ELA class because her students were at such varied reading levels and the text was so complex. Now she has found a way for all her students to access the richness of Shakespeare's story. Ms. Lelle teaches whole-class minilessons on the key ideas, literary devices, and strategies she wants all students to know. Then students work in smaller groups to read the text. Advanced readers read the actual Shakespearean play. Students in the middle read a split textbook that has the actual text on one side and a modern translation on the other. Students who are not able to read the text without support listen to an audiotape of the play while they follow along in the text. A small group of ELL students read a comic book edition of the text that uses pictures and simple language. Now Ms. Lelle looks forward to the unit she used to dread, and all her students have access to Shakespeare's wonderful story and powerful themes.

5

Chew or Process

Multiple means of engagement taps into learners' interests, challenges them appropriately, and motivates them to learn . . . The materials and methods teachers use can either present students with barriers to understanding or enhance their opportunities to learn.

—Center for Applied Special
Technology (CAST) (1999–2009)

Teacher Learning Target

CHEW

Concept: Chew/process

Understand that (key principles)

- Teachers vary the learning modalities used to process or *chew* on new learning to better meet the needs of the diverse learners in their classrooms.

Know (facts)

- Process (chew)
- Learning styles
- Bloom's taxonomy

Able to do (skills)

- Vary the modalities used to teach the chew or the way to process new information by whole class, choice, or readiness.

Now you get it!

- Dedicate one day a week, five minutes per day, or two minutes per lesson to a short discussion with your students about the importance of processing information. For example, you might start or end a lesson by explaining why you chose a certain modality for the day's lesson. Or you could discuss how important it is for each learner to discover their most effective modality for chewing or processing information. You could even explain how dendrites grow from taking on appropriate chew challenges.

Learn a fact today, another one the next, take the test on Friday, dump the information from memory over the weekend, and repeat again next week. We call it "input-output learning." Notice the absence of time to chew or process the learning. When we fail to give students time to process what they are learning, it's no wonder our students repeatedly ask us, "Why do we have to learn this?" The lack of processing time and meaningful connection in our lessons not only creates apathy in our students, but for many, it inhibits them from retaining the information. Processing or connecting to new learning in meaningful ways is essential if we are going to help students store the new learning in long-term memory. Brain researcher and author David Sousa (2006), tells us that "information is often taught in such a way that it lacks meaning for the student. . . . Yet the brain needs to attach significance to information in order to store it in long-term memory" (p. 42). Students may practice a task repeatedly with success, but if they have not found meaning after practicing, there is little likelihood that the learning will move into long-term memory (Sousa, 2006). In other words, input-output learning does not give the brain what it needs!

What *does* the brain need in order to store new learning into long-term memory? In a word, *transfer* (Sousa, 2006). The concept of transfer is not new. Lev Vygotsky points out that the central role of learning should be making meaning. It is the processing of information that essentially enables students to achieve a cognitive transformation, the transfer of learning into long-term memory (Vygotsky, 1978).

The importance of processing and connecting to new learning in meaningful ways is vital, yet this step is often left out of our lessons as we go from input to output, input to output (or chunk to check). Moving from chunk to check is often done to save time or *cover more content*. However, the processing, or chewing, on new learning in a lesson is the step that allows students to lock in the information. If we want new learning to stick, we have to make it sticky!

CHEW AS A WHOLE CLASS

Let's look at the way teachers chew on new information when they are learning together. Imagine that a professional learning community (PLC) is focusing on how to increase the amount of homework turned in by students. The meeting starts with the team leader describing the problem. From there, groups turn to talk about possible strategies for getting more students to complete homework. The groups create and share charts listing the reasons they feel homework is not being done. The PLC leader shares an article from the latest Association for Supervision and Curriculum Development (ASCD) brief about increasing the rate of homework completion. The teams read the article, return to their lists of possible problems, and begin to correlate their ideas with those from the article.

The teachers in these working groups are chewing or processing information together in varied ways to connect new information with what they already know in order to take their understanding of the issue deeper. The PLC leader intentionally designed opportunities for the teachers to do what teachers love to do the most: talk, gather ideas in writing, and learn from one another.

Students need the same kinds of opportunities to deepen their learning by chewing on new information in varied ways. How do we intentionally plan to vary the transfer and processing of new information? Figure 5.1 shows processing strategies teachers can use to help students chew on new information in varied learning styles.

Remember, chew is how students process or *make sense* and connect to new information.

FIGURE 5.1 Chew by Whole-Class Ideas

	Whole-Class Chewing or Processing New Information	Visual	Auditory	Kinesthetic
Science	Groups create comparison charts of conductors and insulators.	X	X	
	After listening to a science lecture, students discuss their thoughts and ideas in study groups.		X	
	Students learn gestures that represent the actions of simple machines.		X	X
	Students look at photos of animals and sort them for similarities and/or differences based on their attributes.	X		X
	Students work together in groups using markers and chart paper to create their own graphic organizers showing what they know about mass and gravity. The organizers are posted on the wall; groups rotate around the room discussing and collecting information from other organizers. They add new ideas they learned from the other groups to their own organizers.	X	X	X
	Students listen to students read both sides of a flash card to determine if the vocabulary term and definition match.		X	
	Sort It Out! Students categorize solids, liquids, and gases (see below).	X		X

	Whole-Class Chewing or Processing New Information	Visual	Auditory	Kinesthetic
Social studies	Holding labels with key events on them, students arrange themselves into a timeline of the movement patterns of allies and enemies from the major events of a war.	✗	✗	✗
	Students think of word associations to help them understand the term "common good."		✗	
	Students discuss how different cultural music from a region or country represents values held by the culture.		✗	
	Students review attributes of a community through **Let the Music Move You**! (see below).	✗	✗	✗
	Students color code information from their notes: Red = main theme blue = supporting details green = interesting ideas	✗		✗
	Students summarize what they hear another student say. ("Giselle, what did you just hear Alicia say about patriotism?")		✗	
	Students discuss how unfair treatment might affect people they know in their personal lives at home or in the community.		✗	
Math	Students act as data while other students describe the groups in terms of fractions (1/2 of the group are boys, 1/3 of the group have blonde hair).	✗	✗	✗
	Students listen to one another explain alternative ways to solve a problem.		✗	
	Students listen to a podcast.		✗	
	Students draw circles around important details from a bar graph displaying survey results.	✗	✗	
	Students write their questions or confusions on sticky notes and post them in each section of a math assignment.	✗		✗
	Students review the vertices of geometric shapes through **Move It, Learn It** (see below).	✗	✗	✗

(Continued)

FIGURE 5.1 (Continued)

	Whole-Class Chewing or Processing New Information	Visual	Auditory	Kinesthetic
	Students learn gestures that represent math functions.	X		X
	Students create their own vocabulary map for new vocabulary terms (how the word is used, what the word reminds them of, relationships, etc.).	X		X
English/ language arts	Students review key literary terms by playing word definition hopscotch on **Move it Mats** (see below).	X	X	X
	Students listen to music with a theme or opinion and make connections to the theme of a book they've read.		X	
	Students learn attributes of a good opening or lead through **Team Talk** (see below).	X	X	X
	Students work in small groups to first verbalize and then create a graphic organizer in preparation for writing an essay or response paper.	X	X	
	Students clap the consonants and snap the vowels of words to cause the vowel sounds to stand out.	X	X	X
	As they read *To Kill a Mockingbird,* students discuss and record when it is appropriate to take social action.		X	X
	Students repeat the **Labyrinth of Learning** daily to memorize the steps of the writing process (see below).	X	X	X
	Students write in reading logs about the understandings, themes, and connections they make to the book they are reading.	X		X

Activities for Chewing as a Whole Class

Sort It Out

Each student receives a card with words and/or pictures on it. Without talking, students wander around the room to find others with cards that would fit into the same category. Once students have figured out their categories, the teacher calls on each group to explain why they are grouped together. For example, students in one group may have cards that say water, soda, gasoline, and vinegar. They would belong to the category, "liquids." Students can categorize anything from parts of speech, to characteristics of landforms, to math problems by equations, and even computer programs by process or function. You could also create cards that have students move to match words and definitions or build varied sentences, math problems, or timelines.

Let the Music Move You

Students receive a card with four questions. The teacher plays music while students move about the room. When the music stops, each student partners with the closest person. For the first round, students find one partner to review and answer Question 1. For the next partnering, students find two other people to share Question 2. Students find three other partners for the third grouping and four partners on the fourth. The teacher brings the class back together to debrief.

Move It to Learn It!

Movement not only helps learning stick, but it's also fun! Have students *become* math numbers and build math problems. For example, they can make arrays by arranging themselves into six groups of four, then four groups of six. Or in language arts, read various types of sentences and have students use their bodies to make the correct punctuation mark that goes at the end. Middle school students can create movements to remember prepositions or longitude and latitude. High school teachers can have students make up movements to remember "rise over run" in math or the rules of supply and demand in social studies.

Move It Mats

If you get a shower curtain liner and marker, you have lots of options for getting students up and moving. For example, at the elementary level you can make a clock face on the shower curtain liner. Then, line students up with a partner so they can see the clock. Give each pair a time on an index card or by using a spinner. When it is their turn, the partners make their time on the clock with their bodies. (Little-hand students must bring up their knees.) The rest of the class says the time. Once they get the idea, the pairs can make up their own times and have other students guess. At the high school level, you or your students can trace the periodic table on a shower curtain. Cards or spinners can indicate movements such as "jump to make table salt" or "jump on all the nonmetals." Think about ideas like "Geography Twister" and "Word-Definition Hopscotch!"

Team Talk

The teacher gives core groups a processing question or task and tells them to have a team talk. Each person has a job, such as leader, materials manager, time tracker, and record keeper. Giving students jobs gives them responsibility in the group. The group works collaboratively to figure out a problem or answer a question. The group discussion ensures that each person has a ready answer. The teacher randomly calls on students by their job title ("Leaders, please stand up"). Then the leaders share their ideas. They can sit down after they share. If someone says what another person was going to say, that person can also sit down unless he or she has another idea to share. This is a great strategy for making sure that everyone in the class participates and shares.

Labyrinth of Learning

This activity is great for learning sequential processes (such as reducing fractions, scientific method, etc.) or timelines of events. Around the room, tape down images, cards, or maps that represent concepts. Cards can be taped in straight lines for sequences and processes or in circles for processes that repeat. Students daily walk and chant the steps associated with the process until they have the concept memorized.

CHEW BY CHOICE

As adults, we *know* what we need to do to make sense of new information. For example, when we are working on a book, Kathleen will jot down key ideas or phrases to reference later. Joy, the artist, will grab the chart paper and sketch ideas of how things fit together. Alicia will say, "Let me see if I get this," as she talks through an idea to make sense of it. The writing process has been fascinating as we notice how each of us needs to chew on new information. We have not only become deeply aware of how important it is to respect each other's need to process ideas in individual ways, but we have also appreciated how much we have deepened our thinking as we learned from each other.

It is essential that our students are taught strategies for making choices at age-appropriate levels. Offering choices when students are processing new information will help learners at any age practice the skill of choosing a learning activity that will help them be most successful. Also as we look at ways to continue to keep the classroom community alive and responsive to all learners' needs, offering various ways to chew on information will give us an opportunity to respond respectfully to the variety of ways that students learn new information. In Figure 5.2 we see how a teacher can actively engage students in the learning process by offering choices.

FIGURE 5.2 Chew by Choice Ideas

	Choice 1	Choice 2	Choice 3
Chew Choices	After watching a video, write key ideas presented in the film.	After watching a video, draw symbols to represent key ideas presented in the film.	
	Answer Questions 1–10.	Answer Questions 11–20.	
	Walk and talk with one partner, discussing the important ideas from a lecture. Prepare to share out.[a]	Create **Charades** with one other partner to show the important ideas from a lecture.[a]	Draw pictures to show important ideas from a lecture.
	Read a text with your partner using **Code the Text** to process information.[a]	Read a text with your partner using **Check Points** to process information.[a]	Read a text with your partner using **Text Master** to process information.[a]
	Take notes using words and/or pictures on a concept map organizer.	Take traditional notes.	Take two column notes.
	Students think about their opinion related to a new law through **In Good Company** groups.[a]		

a. See the activity description at the end of this section.

Activities for Chewing by Choice

Walk and Talk

Give students a prompt on the board, overhead, or PowerPoint, such as "What were the three most important ideas from the lecture?" Students turn and talk to a partner or stand up, walk (five giant steps), and find a talk partner. Students have two to three minutes to talk and share. While they are talking, the teacher floats around the room listening for quality talk. The whole class comes together to process the talk, with the teacher noting quality talk she heard.

Charades

Students create movements or sequences of movements that represent big ideas or vocabulary terms. In science, they can act out different simple machines or the water cycle. In math, they can create movements to represent subtraction, regrouping, finding the square root, or hyperbolic functions.

Code the Text

As students read, they use sticky notes and symbols to track their thinking. They can use ✓ = I get it, ? = I don't get it, and ! = interesting.

Checkpoints

Students mark sections in a piece of text where they will stop reading to have a checkpoint. Checkpoints can be used to share a question, make a point, connect to information, share what was interesting, or paraphrase what was read. This is a great activity to do with different levels of information or readers who read at different paces.

Text Master

This activity is great for breaking down complex texts. Students are assigned a chunk of text such as a paragraph or a page. They focus on simplifying the information in just the small chunk they were assigned. They may rewrite information or use pictures and symbols to help them simplify. Students share their simplified version in small groups or with the whole class.

In Good Company

Students gather with a group of people who have the same *answer* to a question. For example, "Who is your favorite character from this book?" Students discuss why they picked their answer and prepare to defend or explain their thinking to the other groups.

CHEW BY TIERING

Kathleen, the tech novice, and Wenting, a digital native, are both taking an adult education class to learn how to use an accounting software program. After presenting information about how the software works, their instructor, Mr. Franklin, clearly saw that these students require tasks at different readiness levels, and he has designed tasks for processing the new learning at various levels. Kathleen and the others who are at her skill level will use the software to balance their checkbooks. This task is more accessible because it requires fewer steps and allows the students to draw on previous knowledge of balancing their real checkbooks. The task card for Wenting's group requires them to project a company's budget for the next quarter through an analysis of the accounts payable and receivable. The task has been made more challenging by designing an open-ended task that requires more steps and working with unknown abstractions.

Tiering the chew portion of learning can be as simple as asking some students to answer questions that are *right there* in the text while asking others to make comparisons or evaluations. Bloom's taxonomy is a great resource for adding complexity to the questions or processing stems we present to students. A word of caution: If using Bloom's taxonomy, we never allow learners to stay at the low-level thinking domains. Think about your C U KAN and the level of thinking students are required to demonstrate. Support students who have less readiness by beginning with lower-level questions and building up to your targeted level of understanding. Challenge advanced learners by beginning at the expected level of learning and taking their thinking to more complex levels.

FIGURE 5.3 Chew by Tiering Ideas

	Tier 1 (least challenging)	Tier 2	Tier 3 (most challenging)
Chew	**Bloom's Questions**[a]. Students discuss questions from knowledge, comprehension, and application levels of Bloom's taxonomy.	Students discuss questions from application, analysis, and synthesis levels of Bloom's taxonomy.	
	Students are assigned to a station with less complex math problems that are clearly defined.	Students are assigned to a station with more complex math problems that are "fuzzy" problems.	
	Students are given a list of only the essential vocabulary terms for a unit (see Resources for management chart).	Students are given a list of more challenging vocabulary words.	Students who already have mastery of the essential terms create a list of related terms and key ideas.
	Destination Dice! Students work in three different readiness groups to complete tasks of varying difficulty.[a]		
	Students are given the opportunity to try the **Most Difficult First**. If they can complete the highest challenge level, then they can buy time to work on a free choice project or ongoing investigation.[a]		

a. See the activity description at the end of this section.

Tiering the chew portion of the lesson feels familiar to most teachers because we intrinsically adjust our questioning when we see students struggle. The goal from now on is to intentionally preplan processing questions and tasks to challenge students to process at appropriate levels. Figure 5.3 shows chew activities with two and three tiers of processing. The number of tiered activities we create depends on our own skill level, as well as the needs of our students.

Activities for Chewing by Tiering

Most Difficult First

This easy-to-implement activity was coined by Susan Winebrenner (2009). Explain to students which practice tasks are most challenging. For example, in a math assignment, often the last few problems are the most challenging. Allow students to start with the *most difficult first*. If students can complete 85 percent of the most difficult problems correctly, they have "bought time" to work on a choice project or an extension activity. If they are not correct, students must start the assignment from the beginning to build their skills and knowledge.

Tiered Stations

Stations are locations around the room where students engage in learning activities. The students will rotate around to each of the stations in preestablished tiered groups that have been named, for example, the Red Group (high), Blue Group (middle), and Yellow Group (low). When each group gets to the station, they will do the activity in the folder of their group's color. In math, for example, when the Red Group goes to the story problem station, they will do the more challenging story problems they find in the red folder, while the Yellow Group is working on story problems at their readiness level. Stations can also be designed to practice vocabulary using varied modalities, with each group having a different set of words for their readiness level. With this structure, all groups are working on the same type of activities at the appropriate challenge level. Keep in mind that not all stations need to be tiered. Try one tiered station to get started.

Tiered Station Examples

Tier 1. Students identify three different patterns, naming the repeating shapes and sizes. Students share out in a whole-class wrap-up. Teacher reviews the students' work to plan two groups for the next day's lesson based on who got it and who didn't.

———————————————

Tier 2. Students identify one pattern of repeating shapes and sizes and two patterns created from abstract symbols. Students share out in a whole-class wrap-up. Teacher reviews the students' work to plan two groups for the next day's lesson based on who got it and who didn't.

Destination Dice!

Students are grouped by readiness. The teacher provides each group a sheet with six tasks to complete. Each task will have dots on it that correspond to the dots on each side of a die. Each group will receive tasks at the appropriate level of challenge (remember that could be two, three, or four levels of tasks cards; depending what the teacher determines from the preassessment information). The students roll dice to see which two activities each person will complete. The students complete their tasks independently and then return to the group to share their work (see Resources for a student handout of directions and a worksheet template).

Bloom's Taxonomy for Tiering

The following chart (Chart 5.1) of question stems and activities can be used to help you intentionally design tiered processing questions or tiered tasks during the chew portion of your lesson. Remember, our goal is to build background knowledge for those with less readiness and move them up to the learning target. More advanced students can start at the learning target and move beyond to more depth of thinking.

Chart 5.1 Question Stems and Activities

Knowledge

Useful Verbs	Sample Question Stems	Potential Activities and Products
Tell List Describe Relate Locate Write Find State Name	What happened after . . . ? How many . . . ? Who was it that . . . ? Can you name the . . . ? Describe what happened at . . . ? Who spoke to . . . ? Can you tell why . . . ? Find the meaning of . . . ? What is . . . ? Which is true or false . . . ?	Make a list of the main events. Make a timeline of events. Make a facts chart. Write a list of any pieces of information you can remember. List all the . . . in the story. Make a chart showing . . . Make an acrostic. Recite a poem.

Comprehension

Useful Verbs	Sample Question Stems	Potential Activities and Products
Explain Interpret Outline Discuss Distinguish Predict Restate Translate Compare Describe	Can you write in your own words . . . ? Can you write a brief outline . . . ? What do you think could happen next . . . ? Who do you think . . . ? What was the main idea . . . ? Who was the key character . . . ? Can you distinguish between . . . ? What differences exist between . . . ? Can you provide an example of what you mean . . . ? Can you provide a definition for . . . ?	Cut out or draw pictures to show a particular event. Illustrate what you think the main idea was. Make a cartoon strip showing the sequence of events. Write and perform a play based on the story. Retell the story in your own words. Paint a picture of some aspect you like. Write a summary report of an event. Prepare a flowchart to illustrate the sequence of events. Make a coloring book.

(Continued)

Chart 5.1 (Continued)

Application

Useful Verbs	Sample Question Stems	Potential Activities and Products
Solve Show Use Illustrate Construct Complete Examine Classify	Do you know another instance where . . . ? Could this have happened in . . . ? Can you group by characteristics such as . . . ? What factors would you change if . . . ? Can you apply the method used to some experience of your own . . . ? What questions would you ask of . . . ? From the information given, can you develop a set of instructions about . . . ? Would this information be useful if you had a . . . ?	Construct a model to demonstrate how it will work. Make a diorama to illustrate an important event. Make a scrapbook about the areas of study. Make a papier-mâché map to include relevant information about an event. Take a collection of photographs to demonstrate a particular point. Make up a puzzle game using the ideas from the study area. Make a clay model of an item in the material. Design a market strategy for your product using a known strategy as a model. Dress a doll in national costume. Paint a mural about the information studied. Write a textbook about . . . for others.

Analysis

Useful Verbs	Sample Question Stems	Potential Activities and Products
Analyze Distinguish Examine Compare Contrast Investigate Categorize Identify Explain Separate Advertise	Which events could have happened . . . ? What was the underlying theme of . . . ? What do you see as other possible outcomes? Why did . . . changes occur? Can you compare your . . . with that presented in . . . ? Can you explain what must have happened when . . . ? How is . . . similar to . . . ? Can you distinguish between . . . ? What was the problem with . . . ?	Design a questionnaire to gather information. Write a commercial to sell a new product. Make a flowchart to show the critical stages. Construct a graph to illustrate selected information. Make a family tree showing relationships. Write a biography of the study person. Review a work of art in terms of form, color, and texture.

Synthesis

Useful Verbs	Sample Question Stems	Potential Activities and Products
Create Invent Compose Predict Plan Construct Design Imagine Propose Devise Formulate	Can you design a . . . to . . . ? Why not compose a song about . . . ? Can you see a possible solution to . . . ? If you had access to all resources, how would you deal with . . . ? Why don't you devise your own way to deal with . . . ? What would happen if . . . ? How many ways can you . . . ? Can you create new and unusual uses for . . . ? Can you write a new recipe for a tasty dish? Can you develop a proposal that would . . . ?	Invent a machine to do a specific task. Create a new product. Give it a name, and plan a marketing campaign. Write about your feelings in relation to . . . Write a TV show, play, puppet show, role play, song, or pantomime about . . . Design a record, book, or magazine cover for . . . Make up a new language code and write material using it. Sell an idea. Compose a rhythm or put new words to a known melody.

Evaluation

Useful Verbs	Sample Question Stems	Potential Activities and Products
Judge Select Choose Decide Justify Debate Verify Argue Recommend Assess Discuss Rate Prioritize Determine	Is there a better solution to . . . Can you defend your position about . . . ? Do you think . . . is a good or a bad thing? How would you have handled . . . ? What changes to . . . would you recommend? How would you feel if . . . ? How effective are . . . ? What do you think about . . . ?	Prepare a list of criteria to judge a . . . show. Indicate priority and ratings. Conduct a debate about an issue of special interest. Make a booklet about five rules you see as important. Convince others. Form a panel to discuss views—for example, "Learning at School." Write a letter to . . . advising on changes needed at . . . Write a midyear report. Prepare a case to present your view about . . .

The Bloom's prompts in Chart 5.1 can be used to create processing prompts for various groups.

Group 1

Who is the main character? (knowledge)

What changes happened to the main character? (comprehension)

What caused these changes to occur? (analysis—grade-level expectation)

Group 2

What caused the main character to change? (analysis—grade-level expectation)

How would the story be different if the character had not changed? (synthesis—beyond expectation)

How would you have handled these changes? (evaluation—beyond synthesis)

CHEW: TECHNOLOGY SOURCES

- Kidspiration or Inspiration—student-created graphic organizer program
  - www.inspiration.com/Kidspiration
- Webquests (can be chunk and chew) inquiry projects designed by teachers for students to gather and process information online
  - www.webquest.org

Social-learning networks

- Classroom 2.0—Collaborative technologies in education
  - www.classroom20.com

- Ning—set up your own social network for your classes
  - www.ning.com

- Moodle—learning management system for forums, wikis, blogs, messaging, and more
  - http://moodle.org

- WorldPress MU—multiblog management system
  - http://mu.wordpress.org

- ELGG—social networking platform
  - www.elgg.org

- Drupal for Education and E-Learning—create blogs, online discussion, groups, community Web site. No code and teacher friendly!
  - http://groups.drupal.org/drupal-education

CHEW: ACCOMMODATIONS

Gifted

- Gifted students do not need and shouldn't be required to review what they already know. Gifted students need to start at higher levels of Bloom's Taxonomy while also requiring creativity and open-ended questions. Consider connecting ideas to other content areas or other aspects of the students' lives. Gifted students will be more engaged in the chew portion of lessons if they are provided choice and the opportunity to talk with others who process at their level.

English Language Learners

- English language learners will benefit from pictures and vocabulary supports such as smaller words or short descriptions using easier language. They will need to build upon simplified language that they know; however, instruction cannot stop there. Allowing ELLs to solely function with simplified language is a disservice. While we can start with simplified language, we must plan opportunities for them to practice more advanced language forms. For example, allowing an ELL to express her opinion with, *"I think he will quit because he doesn't like it,"* is a fine start. However, we want to amplify the instruction so students will be able to communicate, *"I think he will abandon the movement because he doesn't believe in the cause."* For students to practice more advanced language, they will need opportunities to work in groups with others who will honor their attempts to communicate with more advanced language structures.

Special Education

- Special education students will need a model or target to shoot for in their processing. That means we need to model and think aloud the task we expect them to do. Students can learn from our mental model when we make our thinking visible. Thinking aloud to demonstrate how we came to an answer helps students understand how to process information. In our Inspiring Learners books we call these skills we need to model and teach students the "Vital Know-Hows" (for more ideas on teaching the Vital Know-Hows, see Kryza et al., 2009).

- We can also add prompts to help special education students access prior knowledge. For example, some students may do well with an open-ended question such as, *"What connections can you make between this chapter and the last chapter?"* A prompt to help students access prior knowledge might sound something like, *"The last chapter was about the cell wall. Where does this new information we've just read about the cell nucleus fit into what we know about the cell framework?"*

Visual/Tactile Modalities

- When supporting students with learning disabilities, and especially those with language impairments, think about allowing chew opportunities that draw on visual or tactile modalities such as color coding, creating charts, nonlinguistic representations, creating movement, or constructing models.

CHEW: LESSON EXAMPLES

An Elementary Application: Whole-Class Variety of Chewing

Ms. McGee is designing various ways for her third-grade class to chew on new vocabulary words from the social studies unit. She wants her students to have experiences learning in various ways so they can reflect on which chew style works best for them. They receive an organizer to track their learning. On Monday, the students process linguistically by describing the term in their own words. Ms. McGee has the students listen to one another's descriptions and add to or edit their own description based on ideas they hear. On Tuesday the students create nonlinguistic representations (sketches, icons, etc.) for each of the words and discuss what their sketches mean. On Wednesday, the students read from their organizers in small groups and act out each of the words in a game of charades. Ms. McGee has the whole class play a *Jeopardy*-style game to review the vocabulary words from the week. First, students play with their organizers and notes; the second round is from memory alone. After a week of chewing on vocabulary words in various ways the students are ready for a quiz on Friday.

On the quiz, she asks students to reflect on the different modalities used during the week and write which study style worked best for them. She plans to use the information for designing choice chewing stations the following week.

A Middle School Application: Tiered Chewing

Mr. Purchiss is working on a unit about genre characteristics. The students have been studying the specific literary elements commonly found in the science fiction genre. In this unit, students are expected to analyze the structures, elements, and style of science fiction. He has designed two sheets of group-processing questions. The questions for Group A are meant to build students' background knowledge at a target level of understanding for meeting the standard, "Apply elements of a genre to increase comprehension." The second set of questions begins with the same expectation and takes students beyond the expectation to higher levels of comprehension. The following examples are student worksheets for processing information at various levels.

Group A

What types of literary elements have been used in this passage? (knowledge)

Retell in your own words, what is the purpose of this passage? (comprehension)

How did you use your understanding of genre to help you make sense of this passage? (application)

Group B

How did you use your understanding of genre to help you make sense of this passage? (application)

Could this passage be used for another class or used to help understand another topic? (analysis)

Can you propose other literary elements that could be used to make this article different? (synthesis)

A High School Application: Choices

On Monday, Mr. Kirby has his class take in information about two forms of government through a lecture and a PowerPoint slide show. Today is Tuesday, and he wants to see if his students have locked in the key differences between Communism and Socialism since many past classes confused these forms of government. Mr. Kirby offers students the choice between using a Venn diagram or T-chart or writing two paragraphs about the key similarities and differences. Regardless of the format, the students all need to show at least three similarities and three differences between the forms of government. Mr. Kirby has three baskets for students to turn in their organizer by type so his review of their work is easier. As he looks through each type of processing organizer, he is focused on the same criteria: did students show three similarities and three differences.

6

Check or Output

Universal Design for Learning calls for multiple means of action and expression to provide learners alternatives for demonstrating what they know.

— Center for Applied Special
Technology (CAST) (1999–2009)

Teacher Learning Target

Concept: Check/output

Understand that (key principles)

Teachers need to vary learning modalities for assessing students' understanding in order to better meet the needs of the diverse learners in their classrooms.

Know (facts)

- Multiple intelligences (MI)
- Formative and summative assessments

Able to do (Skills)

Vary the modalities used to check student understanding by whole class, choice, or readiness.

Now you get it!

Look at your grade book. Note how often you provide opportunities for students to demonstrate what they have learned through alternative assessments such as projects or demonstrations. Are you balancing traditional quizzes and tests with performance-based assessment? Do you give students choices on your alternative assessments or all projects based on one modality? Use your knowledge of your students' strengths to plan alternative assessments that allow students to show their learning in ways that are meaningful to them.

In the world outside of school, our knowledge and understanding is sometimes assessed through tests, such as a driving test or entrance exam, but more often we show accomplishment by demonstrating skill proficiency, creating products, and providing services. If we are going to prepare our students for the twenty-first century world, it is clear that we need to vary the way we allow our students to show what they know. We do need to prepare our students for the world of college entrance exams and high-stakes testing, so of course we need to have them practice and grow their skills at taking standardized tests, quizzes, and essays. However, it is also important that we offer projects as assessments. When students work on performance-based assessments, they learn how to work in teams and create quality products. If we balance how we check students' learning by project-based assessments as well as giving tests, we are creating a learning environment that is much more reflective of the world of work we want our students to thrive in when they leave school.

So, how do we decide when to give a test or quiz and when to design a performance-based assessment? Wiggins and McTighe (1998) give us a framework for making decisions about the types of assessments we ought to offer students.

- Is it nice to know or need to know?
  ○ Give a quiz or traditional paper-pencil assessment.
- Is it a big idea or enduring understanding?
  ○ Use a performance or product.

As we are planning our assessments, we must determine what information is essential for students to have as a foundation to building further understandings throughout a unit. For example, if we want to be sure students *know* the key facts and vocabulary they need as a foundation to understanding, we may choose to give a quiz or test on those facts. If we want to see what they are *able to do*, it will make sense for us to expect some kind of demonstration of that skill. If we want them to show a deep understanding of a concept, we may have them create a project or write an essay response to a higher level question. The more clear we are on the C U KAN components of the learning target, the better we can make sound decisions about what we want to assess both summatively and formatively.

Formative assessments are necessary to help us make certain learners are progressing toward mastery of skills and knowledge and understanding of key concepts before they are summatively assessed. If students are not getting the basic facts or are not able to connect the basic facts to the big idea, they cannot move forward. We, as teachers, can then make the wise decision to go back and help students chew more on the new learning. Formative assessments are used to inform instruction during the learning process, thus supporting students' growth of facts, skills, and understandings along the way so they are prepared when they get to the summative assessment. It is essential that we formatively check and have our students self-check throughout the learning process, not only at the end of the process when it's too late.

Formative Assessment: Reasons for Assessing During Learning

- To monitor and adjust students' work
- To give students feedback from us, their peers, and themselves
- To help students develop the needed skills before the summative assessment for a unit when it may be too late
- To help students realistically reflect on their own progress toward the understanding of the learning target

As students gain proficiency with facts, they will be able to make deeper connections, expand their thinking, and apply understandings. As a final assessment of learning, the summative assessment is used for grading purposes and measuring the final output of learning. After a unit is completed, summative assessments tell us how well students have mastered facts, can use skills, or can apply understandings. As McTighe (Wiggins & McTighe, 1998) points out, if it is a big idea or understanding, students can best demonstrate their depth of understanding through demonstrations, products, and performances.

Summative Assessment: Reasons for Assessing After Learning

- To find out what students have learned about a topic and measure outcomes
- To teach students to reflect on their growth as learners
- To evaluate where students are in their thinking and learning

Whether assessments are formative or summative, we must remind ourselves to vary the ways we check students' learning. We want to give students many ways to demonstrate their progress while we are teaching, as well as to show what they have mastered at the end of a unit.

CHECK AS A WHOLE CLASS

We all must pass two important and very different kinds of assessments to be inducted into the world of driving. All of us must take a written driving test and all of us must demonstrate proficient driving skills to the transportation official. This is an example of a whole-class check at its best! Everyone must pass a mix of assessments: a traditional written exam and a performance-based assessment.

When we do whole-class checks, the whole class is either taking the same test or they are doing the same performance-based project. (For example, all students are demonstrating what they know by creating a poster.)

Figure 6.1 is a list of output or check examples of varied ways to assess students' learning. The chart has been broken down into ideas for formative assessments during the learning and summative assessments at the end of a lesson or unit.

Remember, the check is how students can show what they know or what they can do.

FIGURE 6.1   Check by Whole-Class Ideas

Whole-Class Output or Check-Activities by Multiple Intelligences	Word	Math	Nature	Art	Music	Body	People	Self
Formative assessments (during learning)								
Students play **Catch!** to review information from a new chunk of learning (see description below).						X		
Students create an analogy for the concept learned that day.	X	X					X	X
Observe charts made by students.	X	X	X	X			X	X
Thumbs Up						X		X
Four Corners (see description below)	X						X	X
Exit Card (see description below)	X	X		X				X
Look for misconception on students' concept maps.	X	X	X	X			X	X
Check student notes from a class discussion.	X	X					X	
Check student diagrams and labels.	X	X	X	X			X	X
Observe and take notes while students do an experiment.	X	X	X			X	X	X
Check accuracy of flowcharts.	X	X	X	X			X	X
Look for correct information on a graph.	X	X	X	X			X	X

Whole-Class Output or Check-Activities by Multiple Intelligences	Word	Math	Nature	Art	Music	Body	People	Self
Conduct small group interviews.	✗	✗	✗				✗	
Read students' learning logs.	✗	✗	✗					✗
Check students' maps and legends.	✗	✗		✗			✗	✗
Look at student-created timelines.	✗	✗	✗	✗			✗	✗
Listen to students read.	✓							
Review student's Venn diagram.	✗	✗	✗	✗			✗	✗
Listen to student answers after doing a Snowstorm! assessment (see description below).	✗						✗	✗
Traditional summative assessments (after learning)								
Multiple-choice questions	✗							
Essay questions	✗							
Short answer or constructed-response questions	✗							
Matching tests	✗							
Fill in the blank tests	✗							
Alternative summative assessments								
Write a book or short story.	✗	✗	✗	✗			✗	✗

(Continued)

FIGURE 6.1 (Continued)

Whole-Class Output or Check-Activities by Multiple Intelligences	Word	Math	Nature	Art	Music	Body	People	Self
Create a graph or chart.	X	X	X	X			X	X
Record or perform a live newscast.	X	X	X				X	X
Design a display or bulletin board.	X	X	X	X		X	X	X
Make a PowerPoint.	X	X	X	X	X		X	X
Build an exhibit or demonstration.	X	X	X	X	X	X	X	X
Construct a model or diorama.		X	X	X		X	X	X
Produce a video.	X	X	X	X	X	X	X	X
Make a flowchart.	X	X	X	X			X	X
Write a journal, diary, or learning log.	X	X	X					X
Author a magazine article.	X	X	X				X	X
Design a poster.	X	X	X	X		X	X	X
Present a model of how something is done.	X	X		X	X	X	X	X
Construct a museum exhibit.	X	X	X	X		X	X	X
Produce a painting.				X		X	X	X
Assemble a photo essay.		X	X	X		X		X
Create a brochure or a flyer.	X	X	X	X			X	X

Whole-Class Output or Check-Activities by Multiple Intelligences	Word	Math	Nature	Art	Music	Body	People	Self
Publish a newspaper.	✗	✗	✗	✗			✗	✗
Record or perform a song, rap, or poem.	✗		✗	✗	✗	✗	✗	✗
Students prepare Desktop Lessons (see description below).								

Activities for Checking as a Whole Class

Test-Taking Genre Study (summative)

To prepare students to be effective test takers, design and teach a unit on how to think like a test taker and how to develop test-taking skills. A great resource for this is *Winning Strategies for Test Taking* (Densteadt, Kelly, & Kryza, 2009).

I-Search Papers (summative)

I-Search papers are an inquiry-based research process. The term "I-Search" was coined by Ken Macrorie (1988) in his book *The I-Search Paper*. The overall goal of the I-Search is to actively engage students in selecting a topic they are highly interested in learning about so they design a search around questions of importance, using both primary and secondary sources. *The I-Search Paper* combines personal narrative with research findings, so they are written with voice. Students love I-search papers, and they are much more fun to read and assess than traditional research papers!

Four Corners (formative)

Toward the end of class, the teacher poses a question or a problem for students to think about. The corners of the room are designated, "Don't get it yet," "Makes some sense," "Yes, I get it," or "I could teach it!" After a few minutes' reflection, students gather in their chosen corners and discuss why they chose their answers. The teacher can listen to the problems students are having, take notes for the next day's groupings, and use the information to plan challenges for advanced students.

Exit Cards (formative)

On a sheet of paper (half sheet, index card, or just a piece of notebook paper) students complete one task or problem to be turned in before they leave class.

The teacher collects this card at the door and quickly sorts who "got it" and who "didn't get it" into groups. You can also use the Exit-Card template for students to complete a self-reflection at the end of class (see Resources). This formative assessment is used by the teacher to inform grouping for the next day's lesson.

Catch! (formative)

Designate a safe object such as a squishy ball to be tossed between students. Students share something they learned when they catch the object. This is a great follow-up to a discussion, at the end of class or even to wrap up a week of learning.

Snowstorm! (formative)

Students write a review question on a piece of paper, crumple it up and toss it to the center of room. Everyone takes one of the crumpled papers and constructs an answer to the question. Students can hand back their answers to the authors of the questions to check or answers can be shared as a whole class, comparing similar questions and agreeing on answers.

Desktop Lessons (formative)

Half of the class rotates through lessons prepared and taught by students at their desks. The following day, the students switch roles. This activity can be used to review for a test or as a summative assessment after a unit of study.

CHECK BY CHOICE

It was a unique year for the Smith High School Talent Show. In previous years, students were allowed to enter the competition with various talents: singing, dancing, tumbling, juggling, and so forth. But this year, the staff decided that they needed to be fair and level the playing field for all who entered the talent show, so they decided students were only allowed to show their talent through poetry. Since all students would be focusing on the same talent, it would be quite clear who the most talented student in the school was. It made perfect sense to have a clear, uniform demonstration of talent. There was only one problem. Due to the new guidelines, only three students showed up. The show was canceled.

Looking at project based assessments from this talent show perspective, it seems clear that it doesn't make sense to have all students demonstrate understanding in the same way. We have to be careful not to offer projects base solely on *our* learning preferences and strengths. If we really want students to shine, to be their best and show what they can do, we should offer them choices so they can demonstrate their knowledge in a way that is easy and natural for them. Choice projects highlight students' strengths. Offering choice as a summative check is a powerful way to engage students' interests, allowing them to make meaningful connections while promoting their sense of responsibility, independence, and accountability.

In Figure 6.2 let's look at how teachers can help engage and empower students to be more responsible for their learning as they offer choices of assessment (check).

FIGURE 6.2 Check by Choice Ideas

	Choice 1	Choice 2	Choice 3
Check	Choose any five of ten questions on a test.		
	Make a list of short and long vowels.	Find long and short vowels in a text and highlight them according to a color key.	
	Create a visual to demonstrate your knowledge.	Give a speech to demonstrate your knowledge.	Write a paper to demonstrate your knowledge.
	RAFT[a] Plus: Choose your role and format, have the same audience and task.		
	Select a project from the choice menu of projects about telling time. Select a project from the list of multiple intelligence activities (see description below).		

a. RAFT = role, audience, format, task.

Activities for Checking by Choice

RAFT Plus

RAFT Plus assesses not only students' knowledge and understanding, but also their ability to show empathy or look at something from a new perspective. With RAFT, everyone has the same role, audience, format, and task. RAFT Plus offers choices and is therefore more differentiated. First determine the learning outcomes that students must demonstrate from a unit of study. Create RAFT Plus options that demonstrate what students have learned (an average of three to five choices).

R = Role (can be animate or inanimate)

A = Audience (someone or something affected by or connected to the role)

F = Format (choices based on learning styles or multiple intelligences)

T = Task/learning outcome

(the understand, know, and do of the learning target)

For example:

Role = Choice: an endangered species—bald eagles, wolf, polar bear, alligator, gorilla, panda, tiger, elephant, dolphin, whale

Audience = Humans or other animals

Format = Choice: skit/puppet show, song/rap/poem, brochure, newspaper or magazine article, children's picture book

Tasks = Research from your viewpoint and try to persuade society to adopt your viewpoint

Students can work independently or in groups to create self-selected projects to show their understanding of concepts studied.

Choice Menus

Choice menus offer students a "menu" of options for showing what they have learned. When offering choices as a summative assessment, it is essential to keep your learning targets in mind. Ensure that each choice designed for the menu is relevant to the learning target and rigorous enough to demonstrate that students have mastered the learning targets. Note that the following choice menu has a clear focus: Telling time in hours and half hours is at the core of each project. No matter what choice students make, they must all hit the same learning target.

Telling Time Choice Menu	
Draw a picture that shows what you know about telling time in hours and half hours. Write words or a story about a person who has trouble telling time to go with your drawing.	Make up a song or a rhyme about telling time in hours and half hours.
Make a story about your day and time. Act out your story. Be sure to use hours and half hours in your story.	Make a chart of your favorite TV shows and what time they start. Use hours and half hours.

Choice List

The teacher designed the following choices based on the Able to Do learning target that requires students to "Apply the steps of the scientific process."

Investigation Choice List

Select a question below to investigate. Be sure to include each step of the scientific process in your investigation:

- *If we put three wheels on a vehicle, will it travel farther than if it had two wheels?*
- *Will it go faster with more wheels?*
- *Will the tire material affect the distance a vehicle travels?*
- *Will it go faster with smoother tires than with tires that have ridges?*
- *Does the size of the axle affect the distance a vehicle will travel?*
- *Does the length of the axle affect the speed?*

CHECK BY TIERING

Imagine that you have enrolled in an adult community education course titled, "Be Your Own Tile Artist." You enter the first day of class enthusiastic about taking your tile skills to the next level, but you are worried that you might not be as skilled as others in the class. Fortunately, the instructor, Mr. Pedraza, has taught the course several times and knows the class will be filled with students who have a range of experience and interest levels. On the first day of class, Mr. Pedraza discusses skill levels and shows the class three projects that he recommends based on tiling skill and experience.

Beginning students can focus on completing a flat wall backsplash, a one-dimensional project that allows them to practice alignment and spacing. Some students may be ready to lay floor tile for a small room or a bathroom, a task that requires more dimensions and trim work. Students seeking a more challenging project might focus on a mosaic table top that will incorporate design, spacing, and trim work. You give a sigh of relief. There is a project for everyone, at a level that is just right.

When it is time to assess how well our students are meeting the learning targets, we can also vary the depth and complexity of the check tasks, just as Mr. Pedraza has done with his tile projects. Like all other areas of tiering, increasing and decreasing the complexity at the check portion of a lesson will become easier with practice. Figure 6.3 provides some examples of how a teacher may begin with easier ways to tier the check portion of his lesson and over time offer more tiers based on his or her students' needs.

FIGURE 6.3 Check by Tiering Ideas

Check	Tier 1 (least challenging)	Tier 2	Tier 3 (most challenging)
Check	Unit Test *Choose your challenge*[a] Challenge: You may choose to complete five shorter questions or . . .	Unit Test *Choose your challenge* Superchallenge: You may choose to complete one long in-depth question with more complexity.	
	Project is less complex; student has to solve a familiar school-related problem.	Project is more complex; student has to solve a community-related problem.	Project is highly complex; student has to solve a statewide problem.
	Student has to explain a problem from personal point of view.[b]	Student has to explain a problem from the opposite point of view.	Student has to explain the point of view from the perspective of someone very different (age, culture, race, etc.).
	Students respond to Bloom's[b] level: Explain purpose for a science experiment.	Students respond to Bloom's level: Analyze cause and effect of a science experiment.	Student responds to Bloom's level: Evaluate effectiveness of a science experiment.

a. See Choose Your Challenge description, below.

b. See Bloom's taxonomy for increasing complexity, below.

Activities for Checking by Tiering

Task Cards

Task cards are simply 4 × 6 cards with a project or task on each card. Tasks can be tiered by level of complexity for different groups. You can assess any component of the learning target with a task card—skill, knowledge, or depth of understanding.

Task Card Example: Charlotte's Web

Task Card 1. Why do you think Charlotte and Wilbur were able to become close friends even though they are different species?

Task Card 2. How can we use the lesson from Charlotte and Wilbur's relationship to teach us how to become friends with different people?

Task Card Example: Deforestation

Task Card 1. Write a story discouraging deforestation from the perspective of a family who lives near the rain forest.

Task Card 2. Write a story discouraging deforestation from the perspective of a government that needs to protect its natural resources.

Task Card 3. Write a story discouraging deforestation from the perspective of a scientist who is studying the effects of deforestation upon river system health.

Choose Your Challenge

In Choose Your Challenge, students are offered a choice of challenge they want to take on to earn a project grade. They choose from a menu of regular challenges, superchallenges, or megachallenges. Each challenge is worth a certain number of points. They must add up to the number of points required for a particular grade no matter which level of challenge is chosen. Students get to choose the level of complexity of the tasks they complete to show mastery and understanding. While this may sound risky, most students select the appropriate challenge. Rarely will students select challenges that are too difficult. If they do, a little guidance to try a different challenge is all that is needed. If you find students selecting challenges that are too easy, you can move them in the right direction with a simple comment, "We both know that you are capable of a megachallenge. Why don't you give that a try today?"

Choose Your Challenge Example: Surface Area Homework

These are projects in varied modalities. A student might be able to write a poem very easily but must choose from one of the following activities to show learning about surface area.

Challenge: Imagine you can float above your bedroom. Draw a picture of the furniture that you see. Find the area of three pieces of furniture in square units.

Superchallenge: Using graph paper, cut out three irregularly shaped figures. On the back of each, explain to a friend how to determine the area of that object.

Megachallenge: Create a pattern of various shapes that could be used to create a rug. Explain how a weaver could find out the area that the rug will cover by using the surface area of the pattern.

CHECK: TECHNOLOGY SOURCES

- Design Surveys
  - www.zoomerang.com
- Online assessments/quizzes
  - http://quizstar.4teachers.org
  - www.classmarker.com
  - www.quia.com
- Study Island—Practice and assessments aligned to state standards. Assessments can be used as formative/corrective teaching measures.
  - www.studyisland.com
- Quiz Center
  - http://school.discovery.com/quizcenter/quizcenter.html
- Audacity—open source sound editor
  - http://audacity.sourceforge.net (Listen to student example: www.kingsburyschool.org/userfiles/anansi_5803.mp3)
- Web tools for portfolio projects
  - www.educationalsynthesis.org

CHECK: ACCOMMODATIONS

Gifted

Allow students the opportunity:

- To make connections to their life or meaningful cross-content connections
- To be creative and encourage outside-the-box thinking
- To examine different points of view
- To see the importance or the "why" of understanding a concept
- To self-reflect on individual progress, level of quality, and the process of learning

English Language Learners and Special Education

Before the Test

Focus on reviewing the essential concepts in ways that "stick" for the individual student. Help students focus on the important information through:

- Concept maps, study guides, graphic organizers
- Note cards
- Practice tests
- Individual/group review
- Test-taking strategies

- Mnemonics and memory tricks based on the learning styles of the students
- Chunking the practice sessions into small, manageable pieces

During the Test

- Teach students how to manage anxiety level.
- Give immediate feedback.
- Complete one problem/question from each section.
- Provide teacher assistance.
- Provide test modifications.
- Send to an alternative test site.
- Teach self-monitoring strategies.
- Provide extended time.

After the Test

- Retake
- Make corrections
- Alternative grading (modified)
- Thirty questions—test is worth twenty-five
- Thirty questions—teachers grade only the twenty identified as important for mastery of topic
- Multiple grades—one grade for content, one for mechanics
- Give partial credit

Project-Based Assessments

ELL and special-needs students can often excel in performance-based assessments, especially when given choices that provide ways to express their understanding and that work for them. Projects or tasks need to be broken down into smaller, more manageable pieces that are assessed along the way. Have clear learning targets for the project, and have students self-assess throughout the project process to see if they are on target.

CHECK: LESSON EXAMPLES

An Elementary Application: Tiered Checks

In Ms. Beach's first-grade class, students are learning about shapes both in nature and in man-made designs. She selected four shapes for students to identify or create depending on the readiness of the students. She has designed three different task cards at varying levels of complexity as the check after her unit.

Here is her learning target:

Understand that: Shapes, angles, and lines can be found in nature and in man-made designs

Know: Rectangles, squares, circles, triangles

Able to do: Identify and/or create each of the shapes

Task Card 1. Draw and color a picture of each different shape. See if you can find something in the room that has each same shape. Draw a picture of that.

Task Card 2. Look at the four different shapes. Find two things in the room that have the same shape. Draw and write what those things are. Make something that uses at least two of the shapes.

Task Card 3. Draw a picture of shapes that you see in nature that represent the shapes we are learning about. Create something man-made that would be made out of all four shapes.

A Middle School Application: Choice Checks

Ms. Everts is completing a unit examining the similarities and differences of European cultures and how these traits impact cultural perspectives.

For the final project for the unit, she wants to give students a voice and an opportunity to connect personally with the content. So, she decides to design a choice menu as the culminating check of the unit.

Students get to make two choices for this project. First they get to choose two cultures they want to compare and contrast. Then they can choose one of the following projects to demonstrate what they know and understand about the two cultural perspectives: Create a graphic organizer, write a compare/contrast paper, create a comic book or children's book, compose a song or poem, or create a skit or video.

A High School Application: Whole-Class Variety of Checks

Ms. Moluski is making an assessment plan for her unit on the environment. She reviews her understand, know, and able-to-do expectations for the students. She wants to balance assessments between tests and projects. She decides that she will use quizzes to assess vocabulary terms and key facts about types of pollution. Throughout the unit, her students will be working on the skills of gathering data and working in groups. To best assess these skills, she will use observational data check sheets while looking at students' data collection and observing students as they work in groups. They will also receive points for their notes in the final project rubric.

To assess the big understanding of the unit, students will create a project that allows them to apply all the information they have gathered in order to make a projection about the pollution accumulation in their local community and to design a plan to deal with future pollution problems.

7

Pulling It All Together!

Slowly, slowly, easy, easy, that's the way you climb the mountain.

—Manu, Indian mountain-climbing guide who
helped Kathleen trek for eight days in the Himalayan Mountains

Lynn, a third-year teacher, couldn't contain her excitement. "I'm getting there, I'm really getting there! My kids are learning the lingo of chunk, chew, and check. I am being transparent; they are learning with me. We are *partners* in this learning dance." Lynn had been to three workshops on differentiation and quickly embraced the C U KAN and chunk, chew, and check framework. She began trying baby steps, working with the whole class on varying the modalities for chunking, chewing, and checking. She was ready for the next steps. "I want to begin trying some simple ways to offer choice, and I know I need to try tiering the chew part of the lesson at some point." Lynn sat down with a sheet of paper and pencil and drafted out a plan, beginning with a clear learning target. Armed with her objectives and knowledge of who her students were as learners, she looked at where it made sense to differentiate by whole class, by choice, and by tiering. She drew out what it would look like to move seamlessly from chunking as a whole class to chewing in tiered groups, then coming back together for a whole class check.

As Lynn happily discovered, when we know our learning target and know our students, the ways we can vary the pathways of learning for our learners is as infinite as our personalities, skills, and comfort levels, as well as those of our learners. The following charts show teachers in three different grade levels and subject areas sitting down to have conversations about the various ways they can differentiate when they use the chunk, chew and check framework. We are making their thinking visible, if you will, so you can notice how they make informed decisions about the lessons they design. Figure 7.1 describes icons used in the charts to help make the whole-class, choice, or tiered grouping configurations more clear.

FIGURE 7.1 Configurations Used in Planning Lessons With Chunk, Chew, and Check

You Will See	Which Means	Ask Yourself
●	Whole-class instruction/activity	• Over a series of days, did I provide various opportunities for auditory, visual, kinesthetic, and social learners to be engaged?
▪▪ ▪▪	Choice offered to individual students or small groups	• Do students have the skills/knowledge/procedures in place to make good choices? • Are there various ways students can learn, process, or show this information? • Can I offer choices through multiple intelligences, learning styles, hobbies, or interests?
▲▲ ▲	Tiering instruction and activities based on the readiness of the learner	• Do students have the skills/knowledge/procedures in place to work in tiered groups? • Are learners at various levels of skill or understanding? • Can this concept or skill be made more concrete or more abstract? • Can I create clearly defined problems or fuzzy problems to adjust the challenge? • Can this concept be made more concrete for some students, more abstract for others?

SNAPSHOTS: TEACHERS WHO CHOOSE THEIR CHALLENGES

Elementary

Kelly is a fourth-grade teacher who is new to her current school but has seven years prior teaching experience. After a workshop on the CCC framework, Kelly was excited about this new idea but wanted to start slowly. Together we sketched out her first "challenge." She would do *whole-class* instruction in the chunk and the chew portions of the lesson. She determined that offering *choice* in the check portion made sense for this lesson and that her learners would also respond well to having a choice on a homework assignment (Figure 7.2). Kelly felt that allowing students the opportunity to "show what they know" in a way that was meaningful to them would challenge her advanced learners and allow her struggling learners to be successful.

FIGURE 7.2 Getting Started With CCC: Whole Class, Whole Class, Choice

Chunk	As a whole class, introduce weather measurements by having students do a scavenger hunt for key vocabulary, main ideas, and instruments used in gathering weather data. Follow up with a class discussion, summarizing main ideas.	
Chew	As a whole class, students do a walk-and-talk to discuss three prompts given by the teacher: Each partner must choose an instrument, explain what it measures, discuss how those results affect the decisions we make in a day.	
Check	Students can *choose* to describe three methods of gathering data and explain why each is important in predicting storms.	
	Choice 1: Present a poster to the class in the style of a nightly news weather report.	**Choice 2:** Present a weather report in the style of a daily newspaper.

After a little practice and some more discussions, Kelly was clearly ready for her next steps. Before she started the upcoming unit on division, she did a preassessment to discover what her students knew about dividing. What she learned was that none of her students knew how to divide, so she would need to explicitly teach the process of division to the whole class. It wouldn't make sense to offer choice in the chunk part of her lesson. However, she could offer choice in the chew portion of the lesson (Figure 7.3). Then she would do a whole class check to assess students' division skills. Kelly was clearly gaining expertise in making informed decisions about what was best for her group of learners at a specific place in their learning with a particular learning objective. She realized that sometimes explicit, whole-class instruction is the best way to teach the new content. Kelly sketched out a lesson based on the framework in Figure 7.3.

During this lesson, Kelly realized that a handful of her students had quickly learned the division process and were not challenged enough. Since the students' skill levels with division were so different, she knew that it was time to challenge herself to introduce *tiering* into future lessons. Kelly is once again ready to grow her practice. She knows that if she takes it slowly, slowly, easy, easy she will build the skills she needs to reach all her students.

FIGURE 7.3 Getting Started With CCC: Whole Class, Choice, Whole Class

Chunk ●	The teacher explicitly instructs and demonstrates the process of division, with several examples.		
Chew ■ ■	**Choice 1: Writing** Explain the process of division to a friend, using number examples as well as words.	**Choice 2: Drawing** Illustrate how someone at school, at home, or in the community uses division as part of daily life. Give number examples along with illustrations.	**Choice 3: Music** Create a song/rap/poem that expresses the steps of division.
Check ●	As a whole class, the students complete a ten-problem quiz to assess progress of learning division.		

High School

Edward is a veteran teacher of general science in an urban high school. We had been working with his faculty for six months conducting training and planning sessions. About halfway through the school year, Edward was regularly varying the whole class chunk, chew, and check in his lessons and was also comfortable providing chunk, chew, and check choice in his lessons. Because he was intentional and transparent in his teaching, his varied groups of learners were very comfortable with the CCC language, and he had supported them in making good choices and following through on plans. He was really pleased to see that offering choices that targeted student interests got more of his students excited about learning science!

But Edward knew there were still students who were ready for more, even in his overloaded "struggling-learner" classroom. Edward approached us to help him incorporate *tiering* into his lesson design. He felt the place to start tiering was in the chew part of the lesson (Figure 7.4).

After teaching the lesson, Edward was pleased to see his students were happy. His struggling learners came away from the activity feeling more confident because they were able to process successfully with peers of similar readiness. His advanced learners were energized by being challenged from each others' thinking. At one point, a small debate even erupted from one group of normally disinterested students. Edward knew he was going to continue challenging himself to build his "tiering muscles." For the next lesson he decided to try tiering the chunk stage of learning (Figure 7.5).

Middle School

Betsy was teaching eighth-grade social studies and, in baby steps, she learned to offer her students choices and had tiered parts of her lessons as well. She had built a strong community of learners, and they were ready to trust her

FIGURE 7.4 Growing Your Practice With CCC: Whole Class, Tiered, Whole Class

Chunk	As a whole class, the students watch a twenty-minute video on plant structure and function, gathering facts on a mind map created by the teacher.	
Chew	**Tier 1**	**Tier 2**
	Students work in partners to compare and contrast root structure/function and stem structure/function.	Students work in partners to compare and contrast the root and stem structure/function of a cactus and a mangrove tree.
Check	Learners are assessed on their skills of identifying and explaining the function of major structures of plant roots and stems through the completion of a lab.	

FIGURE 7.5 Growing Your Practice With CCC: Tiered, Whole Class, Whole Class

	Tier 1	**Tier 2**	**Tier 3**
Chunk	Two groups of three students each read about lightning from "When Lightning Strikes" (simplified text from Urban Education Exchange (www .ueexchange.org).	Four groups of three students read about storm safety from the science textbook (grade level text).	Two groups of three students read weather reports from the National Weather Service (primary source, advanced text).
Chew	All groups discuss what is *important* information versus *interesting* information related to key learning targets. Groups prepare an organizer of important versus interesting information, including their reasons for deciding what is important and what is interesting.		
Check	Formative check: Each group shares its important versus interesting organizer and explains the groups' thinking for classifying information. As a class, they discuss strategies good science learners can use to find important information in text.		

and follow her lead. She wanted to create a lesson that included whole class, choice, and tiering all interwoven. Here is what she created (Figure 7.6).

FIGURE 7.6	High-Proficiency Differentiating With CCC: Whole Class, Tiered, Choice

Chunk	The teacher invites a native Belizean to present a thirty-minute lecture on the diverse culture in Belize to the whole class.

Chew	Tier 1	Tier 2	Tier 3
	Students use info gathered to fill out a mind map made by the teacher.	Students use info gathered to create their own mind map of main ideas with categories provided by teacher.	Students use info gathered to create their own mind map, organizing ideas as they determine.

Check	Choice 1	Choice 2
	In groups of three or four, students create a skit based on the learning target.	In groups of three or four, students create a classroom game based on the learning target.

Reflecting after the lesson, she saw a few kinks she needed to work out. From a management standpoint, she decided to create a system of color-coded directions for each tier and a specific place to turn in assignments that matched their color. Color coding made it much easier to monitor the progress of each tiered group and to keep track of the assignments. She had two other big realizations as she taught this lesson. First, she noticed that her students were begging to do other types of projects besides the ones she offered. In the future she would add a "Your Choice" option but make sure she had final approval of students' projects. Second, during the tiered chew, she realized the lowest group's graphic organizer was a worksheet to fill out. She felt their chew activity wasn't as meaningful or engaging as those of the other two groups. When she asked the students how they felt about the activity, she found her instincts were right. They didn't like it either and would have preferred to create their own organizer! She decided that next time she would only need two tiers for this chew activity. Here is another lesson (Figure 7.7) she drafted in just ten minutes! Betsy was excited by her own growth, as well as her students' response to the instruction. She was building her differentiation muscles, and it was paying off for her and her students.

How did Betsy create this lesson in ten minutes? Collaboration! She partnered with another teacher, and since two heads are better than one, they

Chunk ▪▪ ▪▪	**Choice 1** Read the text on Canada; take notes.	**Choice 2** Research Canada using Wikipedia; take notes.	**Choice 3** Watch this short informational video the last twenty minutes of class; take notes.	**Choice 4** Listen to this podcast; take notes.
Chew ●	In groups of four, learners organize their collected data into main ideas. The groups then come together to create a whole class organizer with the same main ideas. As the groups continue to do more research, they use sticky notes, to add information to the organizer. Note: Even though they are working in small groups, all groups are doing the same activity, so it is a whole-class activity—there is no differentiation among the group work.			
Check ▲▲ ▲	**Tier 1**		**Tier 2**	
	Students create a top-ten list of reasons to live in Canada (their perspective).		Students create a top-ten list of reasons two people from Ghana and Germany would want to live in Canada (broader perspective).	

FIGURE 7.7 — High Proficiency Differentiating With CCC: Choice, Whole Class, Tiered

quickly developed the lesson and had fun doing it. They agreed to meet afterward to reflect on how the lesson went. Collaboration is a powerful tool for growing our differentiating skills, and it helps us try new ideas that are out of our comfort zone.

SNAPSHOTS: UNIT PLANNING

Now, let's look at two examples of units (one secondary, the other elementary) where teachers pulled together all their understanding about knowing their students, knowing their targets, and varying the pathways to create a seamless differentiated learning experience that works for all students.

Secondary Example

Starting with the end in mind, Hannah thought about what her students should *understand, know,* and *be able to do* in the next two weeks (Figure 7.8). From there, she broke down the C U KAN into weekly learning targets (Figures 7.9 and 7.10). When designing lessons, the sequence of learning will not always be chunk, then chew, then check. Nor will lessons always be completed in one class period. Based on the skills portion of the learning target for Week 1, she decided on a series of chunks and chews before a formal assessment with a written paragraph.

FIGURE 7.8 Learning Target for a Two-Week Unit

English Language Arts Unit (Two weeks)

Concept: Choice
Understand (that)

- People have choices about how they face and handle personal challenges
- The choices we make can affect the human condition in our world (home, school, community, country, world)

Know

- Strategies for effective reading, writing, and communicating
- Essential elements of the story for this unit (*All Summer in a Day*)

Able to do (skills)

- Make connections from text to text/self/world
- Make inferences during and after reading
- Make and adjust predictions
- Use an organizing structure to tell a story

FIGURE 7.9 Week 1 CCC Framework

Chunk ▲▲ ▲	Tier 1		Tier 2
	Students who need more support will read with the teacher or listen to an audiotape of *All Summer in a Day*.		Students who are able to read the text *All Summer in a Day* will read independently.
Chew ▲▲ ▲	Tier 1	Tier 2	Tier 3
	With talk partners, students will respond to question prompts that relate to personal choices, handling challenges, and creating belonging. Questions will be tiered from Bloom's knowledge level up to evaluation level to challenge students at appropriate levels (see Chapter 5 for further examples of tiered questions).		
Chunk ●	The teacher thinks aloud and models how to write a literary response paragraph.		
Chew ●	To prepare for writing their literary response paragraphs, students will rehearse their plan with a talk partner.		
Check ●	Write a literary response paragraph.		

FIGURE 7.10 Week 2 CCC Framework

Chunk	In preparation for writing a personal narrative, students will work with talk partners to share a personal story that relates to the experience of the protagonist in *All Summer in a Day*.
Chew	With talk partners, students take turns sharing their personal stories and asking clarifying questions and further details of each other. Each partner will take notes of suggestions that will enhance his or her personal narrative. (Note: The teacher has modeled peer conferencing and the class has practiced it all year long.)
Chew and formative check	Students will work on a personal narrative topic of their choice for the next few days. Students will submit a draft for formative feedback.
Summative check	The final draft submission is assessed with a rubric.

Notice that in both lessons, Hannah wisely modeled what she expected students to do and gave students time to talk and think together before they had to write. She attributes the quality, richness, and depth of the students' literary response paragraphs and personal narratives to this initial practice in a safe partnership. Hannah has also learned that when she offers choice of topic for a writing assignment, the student writing is much more powerful. When students have a choice, they make more personal connections, which deepen the thinking and cement the ideas, effectively meeting the learning target.

Elementary Example

In this example of an elementary unit, Joseph thought about where the students should be at the end of one week. Then he broke down the learning targets to daily CCC outcomes. He was clear on state standards and aligned his instruction with those standards using the C U KAN framework (Figure 7.11). Below each day's lesson, we have included a Teacher Thinking Snapshot which allows us to "listen" to the intentional instructional decisions the teacher is making while planning the lessons. Following that, we have included a "Students Will Hear" snapshot, to allow us to see (or "hear") how the teacher presents information to students in order to be transparent with his learners.

Day 1 (Figure 7.12) consists only of a chunk and chew. As learners are acquiring information, the teacher will formatively check by walking around with a clipboard, noting how students are doing summarizing key details.

FIGURE 7.11 Learning Target for a One-Week Unit

Social Studies Unit (One Week)

Concept: Inspirational leadership

Understand (that)

- We can help actualize Dr. Martin Luther King Jr.'s dream by creating peace in ourselves, our community, and our world.
- Personal and outside influences shape our cultural, religious, gender, and social beliefs.

Know

- Vocabulary—peace, freedom, equal rights, fair, nonviolent, tolerance, prejudice, racism, diversity
- Dr. King's principles for nonviolent protest

Able to do (skills)

- Read and take notes from a variety of sources
- Synthesize information
- Create and follow a work plan for the project
- Self-evaluate (using rubric criteria)

FIGURE 7.12 Day 1 CCC Framework

Chunk	Tier 1	Tier 2	Tier 3
▲▲ ▲	Students work in tiered groups to read a short biography of Dr. King at various readiness levels (leveled text).		
Chew ●	Teacher will model how to stop at various points in the text and summarize key points. After identifying key points, learners will work with talk partners to make connections and summarize.		

Teacher Thinking Snapshot for Tiering Chunk

I know the students are reading at different levels, and this reading needs to be accessible. I think I will *tier* the chunk for this unit so that students are engaged in the reading and are able to gather important facts about Martin Luther King Jr. I will target the higher-level readers first. What format would they enjoy using to gather information about King? I have a collection of old newspaper articles that would be appealing to most of them. I will bring those in. Now I can work to simpler texts—Internet research for the average readers and a simple biography with main ideas in bold print for lower-level readers.

Students Will Hear

We are beginning a short unit on a very important figure in U.S. history, Martin Luther King Jr., who is an icon of peaceful activism. You will be researching and gathering information from varied resources that are just right for you *so you can all access information about Dr. King's amazing life story and his contribution to society.*

Teacher Thinking Snapshot for Whole-Class Chew

Several of the students are great at finding the main ideas, but they still need to work on summarizing supporting details. I think I need to have them stop at various places throughout their reading to summarize key and supporting points—maybe every two paragraphs. I will model how I do this a few times before they begin reading, and then I will float around to see how they are doing. Once they have their main ideas, they can practice summarizing and making connections with a talk partner. They have been working with talk partners a lot this year, so they are getting really good at this. This will also give everyone a practice run before the following day's group share.

Students Will Hear

While you are reading, it is important to gather main ideas and supporting details and begin making connections between them to see how they all fit into a big picture. Let me show you what I'm thinking when I stop and summarize; then you can try it.

At the end of today's chunk of gathering information, you will spend ten minutes chewing on your new information with a talk partner. You have been doing an amazing job deepening your thinking with your talk partners this past week, so I know you will do well with this today. This will prepare you for more chewing tomorrow when we discuss this as a whole class.

Day 2 (Figure 7.13) is chewing and the beginning of a check, which will continue into Days 3 and 4.

FIGURE 7.13 Day 2 CCC Framework

Chunk	Students will finish collecting main ideas and supporting details from their assigned text.
Check	Students will choose a project to demonstrate their understanding of the learning target based on multiple intelligences.

Teacher Thinking Snapshot for Checking Through Choice

The kids are really enjoying learning about Martin Luther King Jr., and they are really growing their note-taking skills, too. I think a choice performance-based project would be a great way to assess this unit. I will use the multiple intelligences (MI) data I collected to help me come up with ideas for *check* choices that the kids will like.

I need to refer to the learning targets for this unit and make sure the choices I come up with match the learning targets. Students could create a display board that could be shown in the Civil Rights Museum in Memphis, Tennessee, or make a video commercial highlighting MLK day with music, scrolling pictures, and facts, or they could write a song, or rap about MLK. They can all reach the learning target with these choices, and I'll add a "Your Choice" option on the menu as well.

Students Will Hear

Do you remember the multiple intelligences survey you filled out a couple of weeks ago? Well, I did that to find out more about each of you as learners. You each have a unique way of being smart, so I would like to let you show what you learned about MLK in your own unique way. I have designed a choice menu based on your talents and interests. You will notice the learning target is at the top of the menu. Whatever project you choose to do, you must be sure to include the expectations of the learning target. I will ask you to self-assess while you are working on the project to make sure you are hitting the target for this check project. Here are your choices. Decide what is best for you. Have fun!

So now you have had a chance to look into the minds of three teachers who are at different levels of expertise with differentiation. They are each working to find the best ways to engage their learners and help them grow in their learning. As they collaborate, ask for help, explore on their own, and reflect, they see themselves growing in their ability to successfully differentiate in the real classroom. They see the power of varying the pathways to get many different learners to the same learning target.

Pulling it together, Managing it All

Here are some hints and tips for making the most of the CCC framework:

- Chunk and Chew
  - When you are doing whole-group instruction remember, offer smaller chunks (twenty minutes or less); then let students chew or process what they learned in appropriate small-group or individual activities so your lessons are a series of chunks and chews before you check.
  - Some content chunks are most effectively delivered through traditional lecture or a sit-and-get type format. If you decide to do this, make sure you select chew strategies that are visual or kinesthetic to compliment the auditory chunk.

- Check
  - Student Formative Self Assessments:
    - Create table tents by folding paper into thirds. On each side write, "Hard at Work," "HELP!" and "Finished." Have students use their table tents to signal to you how well their work is coming along. (Be

sure to check the finished work to see if it is quality work before allowing students to move to anchor activities.)

- You can also use red, yellow, and green plastic cups instead of table tents to indicate that students are working just fine (green), stuck and in need of help (red), or finished (yellow).

- Choice Check Projects
  - Students must learn to do quality work on their choice projects. Prior to working on their project, have students write down or share with you specifically how they will do quality work for that project type (e.g., Quality skit criteria: We will use costumes, know our parts, and rehearse at least three times. In early elementary, Quality picture book criteria: I made a plan, I used pretty colors, and I did my best drawing.). Because you will be assessing each student on the quality criteria they established, students must be very specific about how they will make their project a quality project. You will need to teach students how to think about defining quality, by modeling how to determine what makes a quality project (see Resources for more information on quality work).
  - On choice menus, give each project a number and collect work by number. ("All those who did Number 1, please turn in your posters at this time," etc.)
  - If students will be presenting their projects (skits, songs, etc.), it helps to make an advance sign-up sheet. Be very specific on how much presentation time will be allowed. Usually, if students ramble on and use too much time it's because they are not prepared.

- Choice
  - When starting to give choices, offer fewer choices. Keep it simple for your own benefit.
  - It helps to give students some examples of what you want them to do. However, don't explain how to do *everything*, and don't give them the step-by-step directions for how to do the projects. When you spell out everything for students, they don't learn how to develop the planning skills on their own. We've found that students can do much more on their own when we give them the chance.
  - Students can be expected to do only one or several choices on the menu depending on the time you have and the complexity of the choices.
  - Allow one of the choices on the menu to be, "Your Choice: Must be Approved by Teacher." Why? Students will come up with amazing ideas when you open the doors for them to do so.

- Tiered
  - When you first try tiering a lesson, it's okay to have just two tiers. You can have most of your students doing one lesson and a small group, either your advanced or struggling learners, working on another tier. As you evolve in your skills, you may choose to have more than two tiers.

- ○ Tiered lessons can be short-term or long-term assignments.
- ○ Tiered lessons can be done alone or in groups.
- ○ You can tier classroom discussion questions, homework assignments, or tests. Any lesson can become a tiered lesson.
- ○ Trust us on this one, it seems challenging to tier lessons when you first get started, but as you begin seeing how your students respond because they are working at their appropriate readiness level, your brain will start to think in tiers. It does get easier!
- ○ Color-code your handouts for each tier so you can easily distinguish the tiers.
- ○ Students will be starting and finishing at different times, so make sure you have a plan for what students must do if they are waiting for you or if they finish early.
- ○ While students are working in their tiers, be sure to float around the room giving them the appropriate support they need at their level to work with the understand, know, and do of your lesson.

- Beginning of the year strategies to prepare your classroom
  - ○ Set the classroom tone for differentiating. From Day 1, words, actions, and peripherals should remind students that "Fair is not everybody getting the same thing; fair is everybody getting what they need to be successful." Your class will be prepared and will more readily accept students working at different levels.
  - ○ Gather student data and create learning-profile cards at the beginning of the year or a semester if you have a new class.
  - ○ Establish routines and have students practice
    - ▪ Moving to anchor activities
    - ▪ Collecting papers
    - ▪ Discussing with learning partners
    - ▪ Moving into groups
    - ▪ Sharing ideas

- Brain breaks (Approximately every twenty minutes, learners' brains need a break, time to process what they've learned. Younger learners need even smaller chunks.)
  - ○ Stretches
  - ○ Cross laterals (arms and/or legs crossing over the body)
  - ○ Energizers
  - ○ Walk and talk (or just walk!)
  - ○ Settling time
  - ○ Music and movement

- Group management ideas
  - ○ *Always* monitor groups by floating and asking questions. Help students troubleshoot. Refrain from giving solutions.
  - ○ Use a clipboard as you move through the room to monitor student performance.

- As students are working in groups, write notes to them on sticky notes to provide them with quick feedback without interrupting the group process.
- Appoint roles for each group member (possible jobs: leader, recorder, timekeeper, teacher getter, positive thinker, organizer).
- With students, develop expectations for working in groups. Create a rubric of criteria, and have each group assess itself at the end of each group work session. Then walk around the room and agree or disagree with groups' self-assessments. You are the boss, so your assessment counts. (Possible expectations for giving student feedback: staying on task, sharing ideas, cooperating, using time wisely.)
- Students who aren't working well in the group, even after you have given warnings, should be "fired" from the group and given an alternative assignment to complete.

- Miscellaneous management ideas
  - The more responsibility students have for their own learning process, the more they will manage themselves.
  - Appoint classroom managers /resident experts.
  - *See three before me!* Students aren't allowed to come and ask you for help until they have checked with three other students in the room first.
  - Rehearse directions for new learning formats with the whole class before asking students to carry them out in differentiated groups.

The greater our toolkit of strategies for chunking, chewing, and checking (collected over time), the more proficiently we can differentiate. Variation is the key, making sure we are providing the greatest access to learning for our students. In the end, that is the intent of all these educational initiatives—to encourage us to create barrier-free classrooms where all students have access to learning in meaningful ways that honor who they are. We must never lose sight of the critical role we play in the development of our students' learning lives. It is our responsibility to grow our teaching skills to keep pace with what we know today that makes learning successful. Remember: slowly, slowly, easy, easy— that's the way to grow our differentiation skills in the real world of the twenty-first century classroom.

Resources

The Resources are designated by an alphabetical and numerical component. The alphabetical component represents a group of similar resources. For example, A.3 and A.5 are student surveys. The numerical component signifies the sequence within the group of similar items and helps navigate the reader through that section.

F. Lesson Planning Templates

Resource A.1

Examples and Nonexamples
of Understandings

A s you design your C U KAN lessons, it helps to use this chart to compare examples of understandings with the nonexamples of understandings.

Examples	Nonexamples
Students will understand that examining the similarities and differences between cultures strengthens the fabric of a multicultural society.	Students will understand the culture of Latin America.
Students will understand that writers let us into their characters' minds, so we can learn how internal conflicts can be handled in positive or negative ways.	Students will understand the plot, characters, and internal conflict in *The Gift of the Magi*.
Students will understand that scientists look for order and patterns to help them understand the nature of all things.	Students will understand the periodic table.
Students will understand that mathematicians look for the most efficient ways to solve problems.	Students will understand how to solve algebraic equations.
Students will understand that artists see inanimate objects from their perspective and create the images that *they* envision.	Students will understand how to paint a still life.
Students will understand that we can make sense of new content by understanding the meaning of key vocabulary.	Students will understand the key vocabulary words.

Resource A.2

Elementary Understandings (K–5)

Social

UNDERSTAND THAT (K)

- When you recognize your feelings, you can help others know how you feel.

UNDERSTAND THAT (2)

- In a community, there is an interaction between the people and the natural environment.
- Whitmore Lake is a type of community.

UNDERSTAND THAT (3)

- Martin Luther King Jr. had a vision of the world where all people could live together without prejudice.
- Every person can help to create Dr. King's dream by creating peace in their own worlds.

UNDERSTAND THAT (4)

- Civilizations often change as a result of conflicts among the people about their beliefs and values.

Math

UNDERSTAND THAT (K)

- *Adding* means *putting together.*

UNDERSTAND THAT (1)

- People made up the idea of time so that they could get organized and plan.
- People made up time as a way to measure how long events or actions take.
- Numbers are symbols that represent different amounts.
- Humans created numbers so that they were able to communicate meaning related to amounts.
- Numbers are interrelated to one another.

UNDERSTAND THAT (2)

- Subtraction is a way to compare the difference in the value of two numbers.
- Numbers have relationship and show patterns.

UNDERSTAND THAT (4)

- Probability allows you to make predictions when the outcomes of events are not certain.
- Place value is a way to explain relationships.
- The more familiar a person is with numbers and what they represent, the easier it is, generally, to see relationships involving numbers.

UNDERSTAND THAT (5)

- Being able to measure allows us to see how things relate to each other (distances, building, covering).

ELA

UNDERSTAND THAT (K)

- Language is a communication tool that is expressed verbally (orally), nonverbally (through movement, e.g., sign language), or written (reading and writing).
- Following oral directions requires good listening skills.

UNDERSTAND THAT (1)

- Letters can be combined to make different sounds.
- Writing words correctly is an important way to share your ideas.
- Sometimes the written word changes because of how we speak.

UNDERSTAND THAT (2)

- Much of what we learn while reading is not explicitly stated in the text. We use a combination of words, pictures, and prior knowledge to understand what we read.
- Students need to know how to bridge their *known* experiences to the unknown text.

UNDERSTAND THAT (3)

- Good readers use their own thinking skills to help them look for clues to guess what a passage is about.
- Different genres of writing have different characteristics. A fantasy story has real events as well as events that are fictional.
- Predictions are educated guesses based on information gathered from the title, cover picture, pictures throughout the text, and the written text.
- Good predictions will help you read and comprehend a story.

UNDERSTAND THAT (4)

- Writers communicate powerfully by choosing powerful words.
- When we communicate in our writing or speaking, there are different words that have the same meaning.
- By using synonyms, writing becomes more imaginative and descriptive.
- Comprehending the meaning of key vocabulary will help one make sense of new content.
- Learners have to find the learning style that works best for themselves to help learn key vocabulary.

Science

UNDERSTAND THAT (5)

- Simple machines were designed to make life easier for man.

Resource A.3

Secondary Understandings

ALL SUBJECT AREAS: Understand that

Patterns

Everything is made up of patterns, and when you know the pattern of something, you can make sense of and use that knowledge.

Community or Systems

Communities or systems are interdependent, and what happens to one part of the community or system impacts the other parts of the community or system.

Change

Change happens over time.

Lifelong Learners

Lifelong learners build and refine an ongoing toolkit of strategies they use to succeed in life.

COMMUNICATION: Understand that

Strategies

Writers have a toolkit of strategies they use to communicate effectively. The greater the toolkit of strategies, the more choices the writer has for reaching varied audiences.

Readers have a toolkit of strategies they use to make sense of text. The greater the toolkit of strategies, the more able the reader is to comprehend and use new knowledge.

Oral communication is a dynamic interaction between speaker and listener. The more strategies we have for effectively giving and receiving oral communication, the more effectively we can communicate.

Interpretation

Experiences influence a reader's interpretation of a work of literature.

Knowledge

Writers write from a base of knowledge about their subjects. They use their knowledge to communicate clearly and effectively.

MATH: Understand that

Ratio/Proportion/Fraction

Everything in the world is made up of wholes and parts. Mathematicians represent this idea in various ways with numbers.

Efficiency

There are more efficient and less efficient ways to solve problems; mathematicians look for the more efficient ways.

SCIENCE: Understand that

Change

All matter can experience change through interactions and applications of energy.

Interdependence

There is interdependence between organisms and their physical environment.

SOCIAL STUDIES: Understand that

Interaction

When people from different cultures interact, they often conflict in terms of beliefs, values, and traditions.

Culture

Examining the similarities and differences between cultures strengthens the fabric of a multicultural society.

FOREIGN LANGUAGE: Understand that

Patterns

All languages are a system of patterns. When you know the patterns, you can effectively communicate with others who speak that language.

Culture

Cultures have norms and beliefs that they follow. When you understand and respect another culture's norms and beliefs, you can effectively live within that culture.

OTHER CONTENT AREAS: Understand that

Art

Artists see inanimate objects from their own perspectives and create images as they see them.

Music

Rhythm can be used to create varying moods in music.

Health

When we take risks in life, there will be good or bad consequences depending on the type of risk we take.

Physical Education

Lifelong health involves developing an exercise program that works for each individual's needs, interests, and lifestyle.

Computers/Technology

Technology is created to enhance the quality of human existence.

Resource B.1

C U KAN Learning Target Template

C U KAN LESSON DESIGN
LEARNING TARGET

CONCEPT (overarching theme):

As a result students should . . .

UNDERSTAND THAT (key principles)

KNOW (facts)

ABLE TO DO (skills)

Resource B.2

C U KAN Planning Guide

PLANNING GUIDE
Preassess: How will you determine students' readiness, interests, or learning profiles before starting your lesson/unit?
Prime: How will you engage the learners at the beginning of the lesson/unit?
Where will you differentiate instruction? Explain how you are differentiating as you describe these sections of your lesson.   ❏ Chunk/information acquired   ❏ Chew/information processed   ❏ Check/information out   ❏ Content/the information   Will you be using a dynamic design for differentiating instruction? If so, which design: ❏RAFT Plus   ❏Choice designs   ❏Tiered   ❏Contract   ❏Compacting   ❏Centers
Chunk: How will students acquire the new learning?
Chew: How will students process the new learning?
Ongoing assessment: How will you and/or your students assess during the learning?
Now You Get It! /check for understanding: How will students show transfer of learning?
The information: Materials, books, Web sites, etc.

Resource C.1

Quality Work Criteria

Following are some ideas to help students define quality. These criteria can be used in rubrics.

Quality Writing Project

- ➤ High-level content
- ➤ Meaningful details
- ➤ Neat/organized/typed
- ➤ Writing conventions followed

Quality Skit or Play

- ➤ Memorize script
- ➤ Costumes/props
- ➤ Well acted
- ➤ Can be heard clearly

Quality Poster or Visual

- ➤ Vivid colors
- ➤ Flow
- ➤ Easy to read
- ➤ Unique/clear message

Quality Song

- ➤ Original
- ➤ Taped/live/video
- ➤ Costumes/instruments
- ➤ Loud and clear voice

Quality Children's Book

- ➤ Colorful, well-drawn pictures
- ➤ Language/content appropriate for age group
- ➤ Attractive cover page
- ➤ Writing conventions followed

Group Work (high to low)

- ➤ Encourages others, collaborates and resolves conflicts
- ➤ Listens well, helps others, shares
- ➤ Appropriate effort, cooperative
- ➤ Inappropriate effort, not cooperative

Work Habits

- ➤ Uses time well, self motivated, effort beyond average
- ➤ Time on task, appropriate effort
- ➤ Little time on task or effort
- ➤ Not working, resistant

Presentation

- ➤ Dynamic and Compelling
- ➤ Interest Holding
- ➤ Not So Interesting
- ➤ Sleep Inducing

Effort and Preparation

- ➤ Considerable
- ➤ More than average
- ➤ Sufficient
- ➤ Minimal or None

Visual Aids

- ➤ Extensive, attractive, enhances information
- ➤ Appropriate number and quality, works with information
- ➤ Few in number and quality, little value
- ➤ Minimal or None

Resource C.2

Quality Work Self-Assessment

Name _____ Unit _____ Date _____

Quality Skill	*Super*	*Standard*	*So-So*	*Slipped*
Listening to discussions and directions				
Understanding key concepts				
Taking complete/organized notes				
Completing warm-ups				
Asking questions when you need to know more				
Being responsible during lab work				
Completing homework				
Studying for test				

Put a star next to the categories above in which you feel you did *quality work*.

Below list the categories in which you need to improve your *quality*.

Are you willing to improve your *quality* in any of these areas? If so, which areas and what will you do to improve your quality?

Area: **Improvement:**

Area: **Improvement:**

Resource D.1

C U KAN Rubric Template Example

Expectations	Amazing	Above Average	Average	Awful
UNDERSTAND _____ Pts	• Shows complex understanding of the concepts • Supports with data from text • Explores related ideas _____ pts	• Understands the concepts • Uses some text references • Explores ideas beyond facts and details _____ pts	• Limited understanding of key concepts • Limited text reference • Little depth or elaboration of ideas _____ pts	• Little understanding of the concept • No or inaccurate reference to text _____ pts
KNOW _____ Pts	• Precise facts • In depth and well supported _____ pts	• Covers facts effectively • Well developed _____ pts	• Valid facts but little depth or elaboration _____ pts	• Needs more facts • Needs accurate facts _____ pts
ABLE TO DO (Skills as determined by the teacher)				
QUALITY WORK (As defined by your group below) _____ Pts	• Met quality work criteria • Unique, fresh, or imaginative work _____ pts	• Met quality work criteria • Creatively integrates work _____ pts	• Met quality work criteria _____ pts	• Does not meet quality work criteria _____ pts

Ways I/we will do quality work for our project: _____
_____
_____
_____

What we did that was quality work:	What we can improve next time:

Student Grade: _____   **Teacher Grade:** _____

COMMENTS:

Resource D.2

Blank Rubric Template

SCALE (Use numbers, words, pictures)

Expectations	*Amazing*	*Above Average*	*Average*	*Awful*
UNDERSTAND _____ Pts				
KNOW _____ Pts				
ABLE TO DO (Skills as determined by the teacher)				
QUALITY WORK (As defined by student) _____ Pts				
WORK HABITS/ GROUP WORK _____ Pts				

Ways I/we will do quality work for our project: _____
1. _____
2. _____
3. _____

What we did that was quality work:	What we can improve upon next time:

Student Grade: _____   **Teacher Grade:** _____

COMMENTS:

Resource E.1

Multiple Intelligences Survey

How Are You Smart?

DIRECTIONS: Below you will find eight types of intelligence. Listed in each section are descriptions of activities that relate to that type of intelligence. Read the descriptions and check the boxes that describe you. Go with your first instinct. At the bottom of each intelligence section, write the total number of items checked. At the end, transfer each total to the Multiple Intelligence Rubric, and see what your strongest intelligences are. Remember, most people are strong in more than one intelligence. Have fun! ☺

Intelligence 1

___ I can hear or see words in my head before I speak, read, or write them.

___ I like games such as Scrabble, Jeopardy, Trivial Pursuit, word searches, crossword puzzles, and so on.

___ I enjoy writing and have received praise and/or recognition for my writing talents.

___ I often talk about things that I have read or heard.

___ I love to read books, magazines, anything!

___ I am good with words. I learn and use new words in creative and/or funny ways regularly.

___ When I am in a classroom, I pay attention to all the written posters and the writing on the board.

___ I have a very good memory for hearing and seeing words.

TOTAL

_____

Intelligence 2

___ I enjoy activities like dancing, swimming, biking, or skating.

___ I play a sport or do physical activity regularly.

___ I need to do things with my hands or by moving in order to learn best.

___ I am good at imitating others and like drama and acting.

___ I use my hands and body when I am talking with someone.

___ I need to move around a lot and change positions often when sitting.

___ I need to touch things to learn about them.

TOTAL

_____

Intelligence 3

___ I like to draw and doodle.

___ I am good at finding my way around places I don't know well.

___ I can easily see in my head how furniture would fit in a room. I am also good at jigsaw puzzles.

___ I remember things better if I can draw or create an image of them.

___ When I look at paintings or pictures, I notice the colors and shapes and how objects are spaced.

___ I prefer learning from pictures.

___ I picture things in my mind.

TOTAL

_____

(Continued)

(Continued)

Intelligence 4

____ I listen to music or have music playing in my head most of the time.

____ I play a musical instrument and/or have a good singing voice.

____ I can easily pick up rhythms and can move to them or tap them out.

____ I can easily remember and/or create songs.

____ I often make tapping sounds or sing while working or studying.

____ I can remember things better if I put them in a song.

____ I can hear all the parts when I listen to music.

TOTAL

_____

Intelligence 5

____ Math is one of my favorite subjects.

____ I like to play games such as chess, Clue, or Stratego.

____ I like to do scientific experiments.

____ I like to calculate, measure, and figure things out.

____ I enjoy brain teasers and puzzles.

____ Using a computer comes easily to me. I understand how they work and can spend time learning about them.

____ I see patterns in things.

TOTAL

_____

Intelligence 6

____ I understand and can express feelings about myself.

____ I enjoy spending time by myself.

____ I like to work alone.

____ I am comfortable having ideas and opinions that are not the same as others.

____ I feel good about who I am most of the time.

____ I have a realistic view of my strengths and weaknesses.

____ I enjoy playing games and doing activities that I can do by myself.

TOTAL

_____

Intelligence 7

____ I have many friends.

____ I enjoy playing group games and team sports.

____ I enjoy working in groups and tend to be the leader in the group.

____ I really care about others and try to understand how others feel and think.

____ I feel comfortable being in the middle of groups or crowds.

____ I enjoy teaching another person or a group of people something that I know how to do well.

____ I like to get involved in social activities in school, church, or the community.

TOTAL

_____

Intelligence 8

____ I like to watch and observe what is going on around me.

____ I think about the environment a lot and want to make sure that we don't pollute our planet.

____ I like to collect rocks, leaves, or other nature items.

____ I feel best when I am out in nature.

____ I understand how different plants and animals are connected to each other.

____ I can easily get used to being in new places.

____ I like to organize things and put them in categories.

TOTAL

_____

Multiple Intelligence Scoring Rubric

Circle the number that you scored in each section of the survey. You are smartest in areas where you scored 5–7 points.

	Weak						Strong
1. Word smart (linguistic)	1	2	3	4	5	6	7
2. Body smart (bodily/kinesthetic)	1	2	3	4	5	6	7
3. Art smart (spatial)	1	2	3	4	5	6	7
4. Music smart (musical)	1	2	3	4	5	6	7
5. Math smart (logical)	1	2	3	4	5	6	7
6. Self smart (intrapersonal)	1	2	3	4	5	6	7
7. People smart (interpersonal)	1	2	3	4	5	6	7
8. Nature smart (naturalistic)	1	2	3	4	5	6	7

MY STRONGEST AREAS OF INTELLIGENCE ARE . . .

_____

_____

I NEED TO BUILD MY STRENGTHS IN THESE AREAS . . .

_____

_____

Resource E.2

Sternberg Processing Preferences

All of us process or make sense of information in different ways. I am curious to know, and more importantly, I want *you* to understand how you think about things. When given a new problem, something to solve or to connect to, how do you make sense of that new information? Below you will find some scenarios. Read the responses to each scenario and check the one that most accurately describes how you would approach it.

Situation 1

You are trying to convince your parents to let you go on a weekend teen retreat. In the discussion, you most likely would—

- ❑ A. Present them with a schedule of activities.
- ❑ B. Make the connection between this weekend and future responsibilities that you will soon face.
- ❑ C. Create a dialogue between two fictional characters in which your ideal solution plays out itself.

Situation 2

You are going to try out for the school play or sports team. Do you—

- ❑ A. Practice, practice, practice?
- ❑ B. Analyze the odds of making the cut and study people who have succeeded?
- ❑ C. Visualize yourself making it?

Situation 3

In marketing class, you are chosen as team leader for a project to advertise a new product for the local ice-cream shop. You most likely would—

- ❑ A. Pull out a legal pad and start making a list of what needs to be done to accomplish the task.
- ❑ B. Contact another local ice-cream shop, and see what they have done in the past for advertising a new product.
- ❑ C. Take on the role of a small child who often comes to this shop, and see the shop from his viewpoint. What would make him want to ask his parents to go to this shop?

Situation 4

You are asked to make a decision for your team about the uniform they should order for next season. You most likely would—

- ❑ A. Make a list of pros and cons for three different uniforms.
- ❑ B. Research current trends in sports uniforms and function to see which is best.
- ❑ C. Create a design of your own.

Situation 5

You are at a friend's house, listening to some tunes on her iPod. You hear a new song by a new artist. You most likely would—

- ❑ A. Ask who the artist is, where did he originate, how long has he been in music, what was his musical background. You want all the details!
- ❑ B. Find out if local clubs are playing this music. Look into who the audience is that is listening to this music.
- ❑ C. Think how you could use the song for a skit you are preparing for science class or how the lyrics connect to an upcoming paper you are writing for English class. You want to incorporate into your life!

Situation 6

You have a major project coming up in your most challenging class. Do you—

- ❑ A. Break the project into smaller tasks and create a calendar for completion of each task?
- ❑ B. Research how others have been successful in getting a good grade on the project and utilize their processes?
- ❑ C. Decide to create your project like no one else has ever done before?

SCORING: Tally the number of As, Bs, and Cs, and read the interpretation at the end.

____ As
____ Bs
____ Cs

Interpretation

If you checked mostly **A**s, you are an *analytical* thinker. You probably like details and thinking sequentially. On tests or assignments, you may process best through activities that involve judging, comparing and contrasting, and evaluating.

If you checked mostly **B**s, you are a *practical* thinker. You probably like to focus on the use and application of new learning; on tests or assignments. You may process best through activities that involve trying things out, putting things into practice, and demonstrating.

If you checked mostly **C**s, you are a *creative* thinker. You probably like to think outside of the box and ask "what if" questions. On tests or assignments, you may process best through activities that involve inventing, imagining, creating, and predicting.

If you found you had an equal distribution of answers, you most likely have several ways to process information. Start noticing when you use creative thinking, practical thinking, or analytical thinking to find out which style works best for you in different learning situations.

Resource E.3

Learning Styles Inventory

Everyone learns differently. Learning styles are the ways that we are able to take in and make sense of new information. Of the six different learning styles, most people have one or two that are their strengths. However, you may have a combination of several styles that you use for learning. Answer each question below with the response that *best* describes how you take in and think about new information. At the end, tally your score, and read the interpretation.

_____1. To make sense of new learning, it helps me to

    A. Talk about it

    B. Think about it

    C. Read about it

    D. Write about it

    E. Hear about it

    F. Work with it

_____2. I do best in classes where teachers

    A. Let me work in small groups and discuss new ideas

    B. Let me have some quiet time to process and visualize new learning

    C. Let me read about new information before lecture

    D. Let me journal about my thoughts and questions

    E. Lecture on new information

    F. Design an activity for me to do; draw, construct, experiment

_____3. If I need to get directions to a new place, I prefer to

    A. Repeat the directions verbally

    B. See the map in my mind

    C. Read the written directions

    D. Write the directions down for myself

    E. Listen to someone give me directions

    F. Grab a map and figure it out

_____4. If the teacher draws a diagram on the board, I make sense of it by

    A. Talking about it with a friend

    B. Seeing the picture

    C. Reading some text that discusses the concept

    D. Writing down the major ideas

    E. Remembering what the teacher said about it

    F. Drawing it for myself

_____5. If I need to learn how to spell a new word, I will

    A. Say it over and over again to myself

    B. Visualize the letters in my mind

    C. Look at it on paper

    D. Write it a few times

    E. Spell it out loud to hear if it sounds right

    F. Use my fingers to trace the letters in the air

Interpretation of the Learning Styles Survey

I had the highest number of _____

If you had three or more As, one of your strongest learning styles is _speaking._ You learn best by expressing yourself out loud.

If you had three or more Bs, one of your strongest learning styles is _visualizing._ You learn best when you have a picture in your mind.

If you had three or more Cs, one of your strongest learning styles is _reading._ It is easy for you to read about things and remember and understand them.

If you had three or more Ds, one of your strongest learning styles is _writing._ You express yourself easily through writing.

If you had three or more Es, one of your strongest learning styles is _listening._ It is easy for you to acquire new information by hearing it.

If you had three or more Fs, one of your strongest learning styles is _manipulating._ You learn best by manipulating objects and moving things around.

    Honor the way you learn. When you are given a choice of how to take in new information, use this knowledge of the strengths you have and use your learning style to own the new learning!

Resource E.4

General Interest Inventory

NAME: _____   DATE: _____

1. What is your favorite subject to learn about in school (check all that apply)?

   ❏ Writing
   ❏ Reading literature
   ❏ Physical education
   ❏ History
   ❏ Science
   ❏ Art
   ❏ Geography
   ❏ Music
   ❏ Math
   ❏ Computers
   ❏ Other _____

2. What do you enjoy the most about school? What do you enjoy the least about school?

   _____

   _____

3. Do you prefer to work—A. Alone B. In groups C. Both (Circle One)

4. What hobbies and special interests do you have (sports, clubs, collections, activities)? Be specific.

   _____

   _____

   _____

5. What do you like to do when you have free time?

   _____

   _____

   _____

6. How much time do you spend watching TV each week? —————

What do you watch?

_____

_____

_____

7. How much time do you spend on the computer each week? —————

What do you like to do on the computer?

_____

_____

_____

_____

8. What types of music do you listen to?

_____

_____

_____

9. What should a teacher know about you that will help you learn best in school?

_____

_____

_____

10. What is the most important thing to you in your life? What are your future goals?

_____

11. What should a teacher know about you that will help you do your best in school?

_____

_____

_____

12. What is something that you do really well and that you are most proud of?

_____

_____

_____

_____

_____

Examples of Content-Specific Inventories

Science—Newton's Laws of Motion

Rank order these categories (1 = top choice) to show what you are most interested in studying during our unit on Newton's Laws of Motion?

___ Car racing

___ Theme parks

___ Machines

___ Architecture

___ Musical instruments

___ Sports (pole vault, football)

Math—Geometry Unit

Which do you like better?

____ Practical geometry

____ Theoretical geometry

Rate the following in order of personal enjoyment using 1 (high)–3 (low).

___ Solving geometric equations

___ Drawing geometric figures

___ Discovering the history of geometry

(Continued)

Examples of Content-Specific Inventories (continued)

History—Civil War

Which topics of the Civil War are you most knowledgeable about?

_____ Causes

_____ Effects

_____ Battles

_____ Heroes

_____ Strategies

When comparing causes of the Civil War to political issues today, would you prefer to

_____ debate   _____ present   _____ perform   _____ write   _____ display

---

Literature—Shakespeare's Life and Times

What would you like to learn about Shakespeare's writings as a reflection of his life and time period?

_____ Culture

_____ Religion

_____ His life story

_____ Societal norms

_____ Geography

_____ Government/politics

Resource E.6

Learning Preferences Questionnaire

How Do You Like To Learn?

1. I study best when it is quiet.   Yes   No

2. I am able to ignore the noise of other people talking while   Yes   No
    I am working.

3. I like to work at a table or desk.   Yes   No

4. I like to work on the floor.   Yes   No

5. I work hard for myself.   Yes   No

6. I work hard for my parents or teacher.   Yes   No

7. I will work on an assignment until it is completed,   Yes   No
    no matter what.

8. Sometimes I get frustrated with my work and do not   Yes   No
    finish it.

9. When my teacher gives an assignment, I like to have   Yes   No
    exact steps on how to complete it.

10. When my teacher gives an assignment, I like to create   Yes   No
    my own steps on how to complete it.

11. I like to work by myself.   Yes   No

12. I like to work in pairs or in groups.   Yes   No

13. I like to have an unlimited amount of time to work on   Yes   No
    an assignment.

14. I like to have a certain amount of time to work on an   Yes   No
    assignment.

15. I like to learn by moving and doing.   Yes   No

Resource F.1

Whole-Class CCC Planner

Understand that: _____

Know: _____

Able to do: _____

Chunk	☐ visual	☐ auditory	☐ kinesthetic

Chew	☐ visual	☐ auditory	☐ kinesthetic

Check

Resource F.2

Choice CCC Planner

Understand that: _____

Know: _____

Able to do: _____

	Choice 1	Choice 2	Choice 3
Chunk 			
Chew 			
Check 			

Resource F.3

Tiered CCC Planner

Understand that: _____

Know: _____

Able to do: _____

	Concrete Simple Application Clearly Defined		Abstract Complex Application Fuzzy Problems
	Tier 1	Tier 2	Tier 3
Chunk *Materials* *Content*			
Chew *Questions* *Tasks* *Roles*			
Check *Questions* *Tasks* *Roles*			

Resource F.4

Varying Complexity for Tiering

Check for Learning Target Using—	Examples
Questions • Literal versus symbolic • Event based versus idea based • Concrete versus open-ended	*Tier 1. Why do you think Charlotte and Wilbur were able to become close friends even though they are different species?*
	Tier 2. How can we use the lesson from Charlotte and Wilbur's relationship to teach us how to become friends with different people?
	Tier 1. Students discuss in pairs why hummingbirds migrate to Central America.
	Tier 2. Students discuss in pairs what might cause humans to migrate to other planets.
Tasks • Few or no abstractions versus multiple abstractions • Problem is specific versus problem is ambiguous • Investigation assigned by teacher versus open investigation	*Tier 1. Students identify three different patterns, naming the repeating shapes and sizes.*
	Tier 2. Students identify patterns from symbolic notations.
	Tier 1. Story-problem example: Alicia had fourteen stickers on her folder. Her friend Zena had twenty-one. Her other friend, Stephen had sixteen. Find the range for stickers they had.
	Tier 2. Story-problem example: Alicia had twenty-four stickers on her folder. Her friend Zena had double that number. Her other friend, Stephen had sixteen. Find the range for stickers they had.
Roles • Narrow range of approaches versus wider range of approaches • Personal perspective vs. broader perspective or viewpoint	*Tier 1. Write a story discouraging deforestation from the perspective of a family who lives near the rain forest.*
	Tier 2. Write a story discouraging deforestation from the perspective of a government that needs to protect its natural resources.
	Tier 1. Students create a top-ten list of reasons to live in Canada (their perspective).
	Tier 2. Students create a top-ten list of reasons two people from Ghana and Germany would want to live in Canada.

Resource F.5

Stations Planning Guide

Unit:

Learning Target

Concept:

Understand that:

Know:

Able to do:

Accountability

Daily center behavior:

Upon completion:

Other:

CENTER 1. Title:

Targeted objectives:

Materials needed:

Structured or exploratory activity:

CENTER 2. Title:

Targeted objectives:

Materials needed:

Structured or exploratory activity:

CENTER 3. Title:

Targeted objectives:

Materials needed:

Structured or exploratory activity:

Exit Card Template

STATION EXIT CARD: Self Assessment					
Name		**Station**			
	Low				High
I used my station time wisely.	1	2	3	4	5
I completed the station task.	1	2	3	4	5
I understood the objectives of the station.	1	2	3	4	5
What I learned:					
Some questions I have:					

Resource F.7

RAFT Plus Template

Understand that: _____

Know: _____

Able to do: _____

Role:
Audience:
Format:
Task (activity):

Choice Menu Template

Understand that: _____

Know: _____

Able to Do: _____

Now You Get It! _____

Resource F.9

Choice Options Based on Multiple Intelligences

Verbal-linguistic (word smart)
- Write any genre
- Jokes/riddles
- Learning logs
- Word games
- Reading
- Speeches/interviews

Musical (music smart)
- Write or rewrite songs
- Move to music
- Create musical mnemonics
- Musical learning games
- Match feelings to rhythms
- Compose

Logical-mathematical (math smart)
- Solve/deduce
- Analyze situations
- Ask questions
- Construct Venn diagrams
- Create or play strategy games
- Graph/chart

Spatial (art smart)
- Perceive
- Draw
- Design
- Graphic organizers
- Arrange
- Three dimensional

Interpersonal (people smart)
- Debate
- Teach others
- Brainstorm
- Lead discussion
- Create group activity
- Organize event

Bodily-kinesthetic (body smart)
- Movement games
- Use body language
- Act or mime
- Move while working
- Dance
- Charades

Intrapersonal (self smart)
- Plan own agenda/set goals
- Observe and note
- Imagine
- Journal
- Reflect
- Create

Naturalistic (nature smart)
- Classify
- Make connections
- Categorize
- Make nature connections
- Create from nature
- Notice relationships

Resource F.10

Destination Dice Template

Destination Dice!

You will be working in groups of three to complete six activities that will help you gain a deeper understanding of our learning target.

Understand that: _____

Know:_____

Able to do:_____

Now you get it!_____

The Destination Dice handout you received is unique for your group's readiness level. Each card on the handout corresponds to the numbers on a die. Take turns rolling the die to determine your destiny. The activity that corresponds with the number on your die will be the activity you are responsible for. You'll each have two activities. Roll until all six activities are assigned. Work on your assigned cards, asking for guidance from your teammates when necessary. Once all six cards are complete, take turns reflecting on the activity, where it brought you in your understanding, and checking with your partners to see that they understand it, too. No one understands until we all understand!

Dicing Sheet 1

(Continued)

Dicing Sheet 2

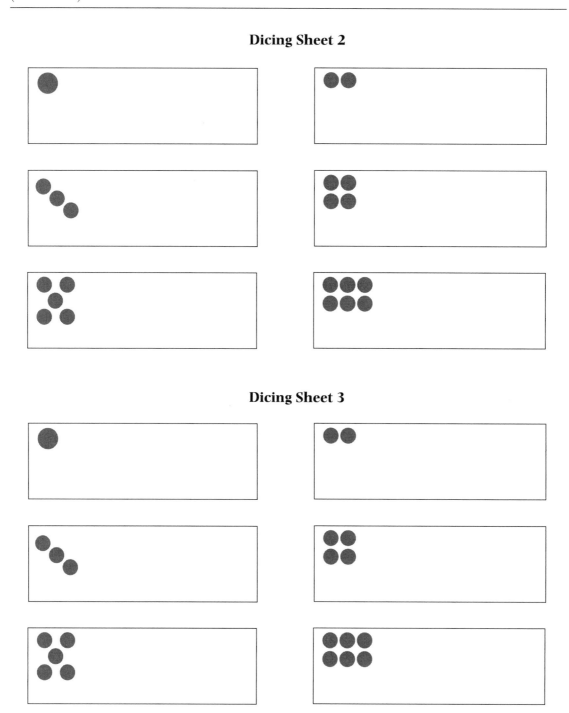

Dicing Sheet 3

Resource F.11

Jigsaw Planning Template

Jigsaw Facts TOPIC _____			
Name:			
Group 1	*Group 2*	*Group 3*	*Group 4*

Resource G.1

Varied Level Texts

Lerner Classroom

www.lernerclassroom.com
Leveled nonfiction books and teaching guides
Social studies, science, reading/literacy
K–8

Redbrick

www.redbricklearning.com
Leveled nonfiction
K–8

National Geographic

www.nationalgeographic.com/education
Nonfiction literacy catalog
Reading comprehension, expository writing, differentiated theme sets
K–12

Time for Kids

www.teachercreated.com
Exploring nonfiction: reading in the content areas
K–12

Pearson AGS Globe
www.agsglobe.com
Middle and high school: high-low text resources
6–12

References

Baum, F. (1900). *The wonderful wizard of Oz.* Chicago: George M. Hill.

Densteadt, L., Kelly, J. C., & Kryza, K. (2009). *Winning strategies for test taking, grades 3–8: A practical guide for teaching test preparation.* Thousand Oaks, CA: Corwin.

Jensen, E. (1994). *The learning brain.* San Diego, CA: The Brain Store.

Kryza, K., Stephens, S. J., & Duncan, A. (2007). *Inspiring middle and secondary learners: Honoring differences and creating community through differentiating instructional practices.* Thousand Oaks, CA: Corwin.

Kryza, K., Stephens, S. J., & Duncan, A. (2009). *Inspiring elementary learners: Nurturing the whole child in a differentiated classroom.* Thousand Oaks, CA: Corwin.

Macrorie, K. (1988). *The I-search paper.* Portsmouth, NH: Boynton/Cook.

Sousa, D. (2006). *How the brain learns.* Thousand Oaks, CA: Corwin.

Tomlinson, C. A., & McTighe, J. (2006). *Integrating differentiated instruction and understanding by design: Connecting content and kids.* Alexandria, VA: Association for Supervision and Curriculum Development.

Truss, L. (2006). *Eats, shoots and leaves: Why commas really do make a difference.* New York: Putnam.

Vygotsky, L. (1978). *Mind in society: The development of higher psychological processes.* Cambridge, MA: Harvard University Press.

Wenglinsky, H. (2002, February 13). How schools matter: The link between teacher classroom practices and student academic performance. *Education Policy Analysis Archives, 10,* 12. Retrieved from http://epaa.asu.edu/epaa/v10n12/

Wiggins, G., & McTighe, J. (1998). *Understanding by design.* Alexandria, VA: Association for Supervision and Curriculum Development.

Index

CORWIN

A SAGE Company

The Corwin logo—a raven striding across an open book—represents the union of courage and learning. Corwin is committed to improving education for all learners by publishing books and other professional development resources for those serving the field of PreK–12 education. By providing practical, hands-on materials, Corwin continues to carry out the promise of its motto: **"Helping Educators Do Their Work Better."**